The Enemy Is Us

HOW TO DEFEAT DRUG ABUSE AND END THE "WAR ON DRUGS"

Robert H. Dowd
Lieutenant Colonel, USAF-Ret.

First Edition  W9-CWD-902

THE HEFTY PRESS
Miami, Florida

All rights reserved under International and Pan American Copyright
Conventions. Published in the United States by The Hefty Press, Post
Office Box 56-2075, Miami, FL 33256-2075.

Cataloging-in-Publication Data

Dowd, Robert H.
     The enemy is us : how to defeat drug abuse and end the war on drugs /
Robert H. Dowd.—1st ed.

     ISBN 0-9653999-7-4 (HC)
     ISBN 0-9653999-8-2 (pbk)
     1. Narcotics, Control of—United States. 2. Drug Abuse—United
States. 3. Drug addicts—Prevention and Rehabilitation—United States.
4. Narcotics, Control of—United States—History.
I. Title
Library of Congress Catalog Card Number : 96-94697

Manufactured in the United States of America
9 8 7 6 5 4 3 2
                              First Edition

Dedicated

to

ROSEMARY

My sweetheart since age 15

My wife of 55 years

ACKNOWLEDGEMENTS

Dr. Robert H. Schuller was unaware of his role, but he must be credited for providing the motivating force to launch this book. As a regular listener to his *Hour of Power* weekly television sermons from the Crystal Cathedral in Garden Grove, California, I was moved to action by his constant prodding to act upon the ideas that the Lord continually gives us. When Dr. Schuller said, "If you do not act upon your good ideas, nothing will happen," I listened. But when he thundered, *"If it is going to be, it is up to me!"* I began writing.

Then, I was dealt a winning hand of four Jacks—four friends, all named Jack, who were the prime movers in the creation of this book:

Jack Schenkman—a man who has lived the American dream of a young immigrant boy rising to a position of wealth and influence—to whom I first revealed my intentions to write this book. His enthusiasm and assistance has been most helpful and a source of continuous encouragement.

Jack Stark—a long time writer for the Miami Herald and an author of several books—looked over my early manuscripts and offered much professional advice and support.

Jack Norton—Colonel, USA-Ret. and an attorney—was an invaluable asset because of his extensive military background as a paratrooper in WW II, a Platoon Leader in Korea, and later a senior Judge Advocate in Vietnam. His criticisms were constructive, demanding, and perceptive.

Jack Pickering—my Editor—what more can I say? His years of experience in some of the best publishing firms in New York City, and later as the Editorial Director at Pennsylvania State University Press, provided a steady hand on the tiller as we steered this project to its completion. Not that there was not some choppy water to navigate in the clash of perspectives of an Eastern liberal intellectual and a military conservative. While we often disagreed, our relationship never became disagreeable, and even after this experience we remain respectful of each other's position as well as good friends.

Always at my side was my pal since boyhood, **Judge Ray Pearson**, as was my family, **wife Rosemary,** and **sons Lt. Col.-Ret. Robert M. and Maj. James W.**, both of the USAF. All read countless passages and made significant suggestions as to how I might improve the sense of my thoughts.

My thanks to **Maj. Gen. John Moench** for his suggestions on packaging the product and the content of the text on the dust cover. And I certainly don't want to overlook the contributions of **Joseph and Marilynn Shepherd**. The jacket design was Joe's idea and Marilynn assisted in a hundred different ways over the past five years. Thanks to all my unmentioned friends and family for the thousands of little things that helped the process along.

David F. Musto, MD must be acknowledged as the authority on the history of narcotics control in the United States and applauded for his outstanding book *The American Disease—Origins of Narcotic Control.* It would seem impossible to write anything on drug control without constantly referring to the excellent research of Dr. Musto, which I have done liberally in my book.

I arrived at my position on drug control in the United States over time, and was pleased to find that my thinking was in line with that of *Milton Friedman, Nobel laureate in economics,* whom I consider to be one of the best minds of our generation. We are all indebted to this gentleman for his many contributions to our society.

CONTENTS

1

THE SITUATION BRIEFING

"I have met the enemy and he is us," proclaimed Pogo to his compatriots of the Okefenokee Swamp. The homeland of Walt Kelly's cartoon characters had apparently been invaded by aliens, and Pogo was delegated to search out this unseen but ubiquitous enemy. Everyone in the swamp community was reacting in panic at every shadow and sound. While reconnoitering, Pogo observed the critters of the Okefenokee, one and then another, fleeing in terror through the swamp in every direction, yet he saw no sign of an enemy. He soon realized that in their panic the critters were the ones causing the commotion. Tranquillity once again returned to their little community in the swamp after Pogo calmed their fears by convincing them that there was no enemy.[1]

In the "War on Drugs," Americans are like Walt Kelly's swamp critters of the Okefenokee, charging through the Andean Jungles of South America and the Asphalt Jungles of America's inner cities searching for the enemy. Government officials point to drug traffickers—foreign and domestic—as the enemy. But the enemy is us—those among us who create the demand for illegal drugs by buying the drug dealers' wares. The government's hope of eliminating recreational drug use by shutting off the supply of drugs to deny its citizens access to narcotics and cocaine has proved to be an ill-conceived strategy. Not only is this method ineffective, it is the cause of the drug morass in the United States.

Despite the world-wide growth, power, and criminal influence of the illegal drug cartels, Congress sustains prohibition—the very thing that makes drug smuggling a profitable venture. Government agents then do battle throughout the world with the drug lords and their minions. What is most curious, Americans are heavily taxed to support the War on Drugs, even while those citizens that the U.S. government is attempting to protect from their unwise behavior eagerly buy the smuggler's goods. Profits from those drug sales then finance the drug cartels' battle with the authorities. It is painfully evident that Americans are financing both sides in the War on Drugs. Pogo would say, "The Enemy Is Us."

The Enemy Is Us

Destroying drug crops and attacking drug trafficking in producing nations is a failed strategy that originated with the Theodore Roosevelt administration when it tried to enforce a ban on opium smoking in the newly acquired Philippine Islands. That strategy was resurrected by President Nixon for his War on Drugs and has remained the core strategy for every successive administration. Despite the government's determined efforts, the supply of illegal drugs has saturated the underground drug market for years. Yale University's medical historian David F. Musto calculated that the street price of cocaine is relatively cheaper in today's illegal market than it was in the legal market of 1910.[2] Yet the Clinton administration tries to force this flawed strategy to succeed by increasing the drug budget and intensifying the drug war.

In the 11th Century, the corpse of El Cid was clad in armor and mounted on his war horse to lead the Spanish forces in battle against the Moors, who fled in terror at the sight of this mighty warrior. The President has reversed those roles, and sent America's military combat hero Gen. Barry R. McCaffrey to lead the charge in the War on Drugs astride a mount named *Prohibition* that died in 1933. Even the mightiest of drug warriors can not prevail astride a dead horse. The strategy to enforce drug prohibition by shutting off the supply of drugs has never been successful in its ninety-year history, yet the general believes that he can make it work, perhaps in five years.

Drugs in the first two decades of this century provide a challenging comparison for today's drug problem. It was a time that an individual could still legally obtain drugs for personal use, yet drug addiction rates were in a sustained steady decline despite active advertising and promotion by sellers. Drug crime was negligible. But defenders of prohibition never acknowledge these facts. Nor do they mention that there are three times as many drug addicts per capita in America today than there were before prohibition. The falling rate in drug use during the early decades is attributed to the societal intolerance toward casual drug users, public health education, and factual information—such as that provided by the Pure Food and Drug Act. It was persuasion, not prohibition!

The defenders of the status quo say the repeal of prohibition would quadruple the horrors of drug use, such as addictions, creation of dysfunctional families, cocaine-babies, and deaths from overdose. But the record shows that the horrors to which they refer are occurring with greater frequency under prohibition. Illegal drugs are readily available

4

to anyone, including juveniles. The steady flow of illegal drugs onto America's streets has made prohibition moot. One writer noted that it is painful and a little awkward for our elected officials to admit to this truth when the text of the Anti-Drug Abuse Act of 1988 sets as the government's goal a drug-free America by 1995.

The War on Drugs is a holy war against Evil in the eyes of the drug bureaucracy. Despite evidence that drug use, drug profits, and drug crime increased even as the drug war expanded, to question its value is equivalent to supporting drug abuse. Many concerned Americans believe that prohibition is a flawed strategy and that there are better tactics for reducing drug abuse. Our experience with both alcohol and tobacco proves the point. Either of these two addictive psychoactive drugs have proved to be more deadly than all the other psychoactive drugs combined. The United States has had success in reducing the use and harmful effects of both alcohol and tobacco while they remain for sale in the legal private sector. Education, not prohibition, is the weapon our government chose against tobacco and alcohol. And it is working with almost universal support by the citizenry.

The drug war targets the supply of drugs, but it has not reduced the illegal drug supply one iota. When societal values changed in the 1960s and Americans demanded more drugs, an abundant supply of marijuana, cocaine, and heroin magically appeared. Prohibition laws were no deterrent to drug use, and law enforcement could not prevent the plethora of drugs on our streets. General McCaffrey said "that reduction in demand for drugs would be the country's top priority"—and this author adds, it should be the *only* priority. The War on Drugs is a real, but unrecognized, impediment to demand-reduction programs. The drug subculture tries to undo the best efforts of parents, teachers, and health care professionals to educate America's youth for a drug free life. It has been shown that Americans can reduce addictive psychoactive drug-use in a legitimate drug market. We can push reduction of drug-use even further by embracing the traditional moral values of our Judeo-Christian heritage and instructing our children in those values by example.

Prohibition: Panacea or Pandora's Box? This is a parody of Joseph Califano's White Paper #1 entitled, *Legalization: Panacea or Pandora's Box?*[3] Califano tries to defend the status quo in his paper by suggesting that terrible things would happen should drugs be legalized. The parody provides the proper perspective to this discussion of drug policy. *Prohibition* is the subject on trial. A legitimate drug market is the norm in the free enterprise system, as it was for the first 144 years of this nation. The teetotalers in the Temperance movement advocated prohibition as the panacea for society's problem with drunks and dope fiends. However, the United States opened Pandora's box with alcohol and drug prohibition in 1920. This nation now endures the crime, violence, and corruption from drug trafficking that did not exist in the days of legal narcotics and cocaine—and it still has a drug problem that is greater than in preprohibition days.

There are many ironies in the history of drug control, but none more mocking than the premise upon which drug prohibition was framed. The Harrison Narcotics Act of 1914 permitted doctors to prescribe narcotics for medical purposes, and for the next five years most addicts were maintained in their habit by their doctors. The Internal Revenue Service (IRS) interpreted the law as prohibiting narcotics to maintain an addict since addiction is not a disease—therefore, this was not a "good faith" practice of medicine. The Supreme Court rejected the IRS argument in 1916. But in the exhilaration of a successful national movement for alcohol prohibition, the Court reversed itself in 1919 and upheld the IRS position. Drug prohibition became law the following year. However, in recent years the Supreme Court has held that addiction is a disease, and that addicts are entitled to Social Security disability payments. Street addicts across this nation are now enabled by monthly checks from the government to sustain their addiction.

It is unlikely that those earlier legislators would have voted for prohibition had they foreseen the unintended consequences of their actions. The unexpected outcome of alcohol prohibition became so onerous that Americans repealed Prohibition in 1933. But the catastrophic side effects of drug prohibition did not become a major problem until the explosion of drug use in the 1960's. The drug cartels have grown into a globe-spanning international crime syndicate with revenues estimated at $500 billion, exceeding even those of the international oil trade.[4] How long will the world tolerate such a criminal enterprise that corrupts international commerce and national institutions?

The Book. This study examines the strategy and objectives of the United States' War on Drugs from a military perspective. It also determines the effectiveness of government drug policy in accomplishing the assigned goals and objectives. The drug war strategy is compared to other political and military strategies used in past conflicts involving the United States. The reader may question whether the War on Drugs is a true military engagement. An analysis of the scope, cost, intensity, and expanse of the involvement of the U.S. armed forces and paramilitary units of other U.S. agencies leaves no doubt that it is a full-fledged shooting war. From a small beginning in 1905, the United States has fought an unnecessary but steadily expanding drug war for nearly a century.

The problem periods in drug history are high-lighted. The reader will be able to clearly see points on that path where well-intentioned decisions created unintended results. Strategies failed to achieve their objectives, but government officials only increased their efforts with quixotical determination. Drug prohibition requires an authoritarian bureaucracy that operates like a police state, imposing penalties and confiscating property to enforce compliance.

The book goes well beyond the proposed repeal of prohibition and the return to a legal drug market in the private sector. Remember that a legal private-sector drug market alone would eliminate the worst element of the drug problem—illegal drug trafficking with its crime, violence, killings, juvenile drug-gangs, and corruption. But the book also presents a plan for manufacturing, distributing, and selling generic heroin, cocaine, and other designated drugs that would be freely available to any citizen over 21 years of age. The author does not accept the Libertarian philosophy of a market completely unfettered by government regulation, but proposes thoughtful regulations that would discourage underage sales and intemperate use. The idea is not only to eliminate illegal drug trafficking, but to provide a wholesome environment, absent of criminals, that would permit our demand-reduction programs to work.

Demand-reduction programs should be uncoupled from the War on Drugs. Their success does not depend upon this nation's ability to suppress the supply of illegal drugs. The United States would then only have to contend with drug abusers and drug addicts in the arena of public health. As frustrating as drug addicts can be, we must exercise patience, for people can overcome addiction to return to the world of the living. But the greatest effort should be reserved for the prevention of drug use. General McCaffrey is right on target with his statement on the demand-side of the drug equation. "At the end of the day, there can be only one clear priority and that is focus on youth, drug prevention and education. We've got to tell our children, the parents, the schoolteachers, the coaches, that it's wrong."

Programs to reduce the demand for drugs can be successful regardless of the amount or availability of drugs, whether legal or illegal. The demand reduction programs that show the most promise are based on Judeo-Christian values that emphasize character, education, and individual responsibility. The plan outlined in this book regulates drug use as a public health concern and not as a law enforcement problem. The strategy to persuade and educate individuals to avoid destructive behavior has—in past legal markets—led to reduced drug use. Americans can confidently accept this proposed drug policy knowing that it was effective in this nation before prohibition, and it is also verified by the experience of the United States with the use and control of other harmful but legal substances, such as tobacco and alcohol

A legal drug market will save the taxpayers annual taxes of over $40-billion spent on the enforcement of drug laws at all levels of government. It can raise an additional $20 billion in drug taxes annually to fund demand-reduction programs in research, rehabilitation, treatment, and prevention. This nation would also be relieved of the corruption and disruptions to normal commerce caused by illegal drugs, as well as the embarrassment of pressuring other nations to fight America's drug war.

The supporters of the status quo have created such a phobia about addictive psychoactive drugs that they have paralyzed elected officials' ability to even discuss the matter. Timid politicians seem to develop backbone only when public opinion supports their position. Overwhelming evidence has been found that illegal drug trafficking to circumvent drug prohibition is the major cause of crime in the United States. My investigation found little evidence to support the Drug Enforcement Administration's position that *drugs cause crime.* Nobel laureate Milton Friedman was asked, "What is the one thing you would do to improve the crime situation in this nation?" Without hesitation, he answered, "I would stop the War on Drugs."

The drug warriors appear happy to promote the philosophy that only their efforts hold the "drug menace" at bay. Without public belief in that tenet and political support for it, drug prohibition would be repealed in a minute. That action would, of course, end the bureaucrats' careers, power, and influence. It becomes necessary, then, for those who would change policy to first build public support for that change. That must start with the public's understanding and acknowledgment that current drug policy has created a far worse problem than that which existed before the initiation of drug prohibition.

A few prominent Americans have long advocated the repeal of drug prohibition. In addition to the aforementioned Economics Professor Milton Friedman, there is former Secretary of State George Shultz, former police chief Joseph McNamara, and commentator William Buckley, on the conservative side. Recently two other well-known persons have expressed doubt about drug prohibition. One is the new governor of New Mexico, Gary Johnson; the other is columnist Paul Harvey. In the latter's column, he describes how "the top international policeman, Secretary General Raymond Kendall of Interpol, is appealing for the decriminalization of drugs."[i] The only incumbent national political office holder, either conservative or liberal, to buck the official line and suggest legalizing drugs was the former Surgeon General Joycelyn Elders. She was almost unanimously criticized by the nation's elected officials. Yet it was barely eighteen-months later that House Speaker Newt Gingrich, after expressing disgust with the wide-spread use of psychoactive drugs, concluded that the United States should "either legalize them or get rid of them."[ii] It should not be lost on the reader that this is the first elected federal official to even hint that the legalization of drugs might be an option.

On June 20, 1995, commentator Walter Cronkite called for President Clinton to appoint a "gilt-edged" commission to study national drug policy, similar to the Wickersham commission on Prohibition in 1929. "Uncle Walter" did so on a special Cronkite Report entitled "The Drug Dilemma: War or Peace," on the Discovery TV channel. Mr. Cronkite will probably not be alone in calling for a commission. This is the usual refuge of lawmakers when faced with a difficult decision. President Herbert Hoover confronted the fact that law enforcement of alcohol prohibition was not working by appointing a prestigious eleven-man commission, under the chairmanship of George W. Wickersham, to study the problem. It is worth pausing for a moment from our travails with drug prohibition to recall the words of the philosopher George Santayana: "Those who cannot remember the past are condemned to repeat it." A look back at the workings of that commission reveals that a 19-month effort produced no decision.

Frederick Lewis Allen wrote his informal history of the Nineteen Twenties during the throes of the debate in 1931 over continuing

Prohibition.   His comments on the Wickersham commission are pertinent to America's predicament today:

> [The Wickersham report] represented the findings of a group of intelligent and presumably impartial people with regard to one of the critical problems of the nineteen-twenties. ...[T]he complete text revealed very clearly the sorry inability of the enforcement staff to dry up the country. ...But the commission as a whole cast its vote for further trial, contenting itself with suggesting a method of modification if time proved that the experiment was a failure. The confusing effect of the report was neatly satirized....in the New York World:
>> Prohibition is an awful flop.
>> We like it.
>> It can't stop what it's meant to stop.
>> We like it.
>> It's left a trail of graft and slime,
>> It's filled our land with vice and crime,
>> It don't prohibit worth a dime,
>>> Nevertheless we're for it.

Historian Allen continued with this pungent comment:

> Yet if the Wickersham report was confusing, this was highly appropriate; for so also was the situation with which it dealt. Although it seemed reasonably clear to an impartial observer that the country had chosen the wrong road in 1917-20, legislating with a sublime disregard for elementary chemistry—which might have taught it how easily alcohol may be manufactured—and for elementary psychology—which might have suggested that common human impulses are not easily suppressed by fiat—it was nevertheless very far from clear how the country could best extricate itself from the morass into which it had so blithely plunged. ...No problem which had ever faced the United States had seemed more nearly insoluble.[7]

Two years after Allen wrote that despairing account the United States had neatly extricated itself from the alcohol morass by repealing Prohibition, and the nation has never looked back. The lesson of history is before us—we can ignore it and remain mired in the drug morass, or we can repeal drug prohibition and move onto the high ground. The hypocrisy of the drug war—in both those who circumvent the law and those who enforce the law—is creating a climate of cynicism and disrespect for the traditional moral values of America. While your author applauds the esteemed Mr. Cronkite for showing the seriousness of the nation's dilemma, he sees no need for a commission. The author is confident enough to feel that this book—using objective-oriented military planning—outlines a winning strategy for the War on Drugs.

2

KNOWING THE ENEMY
How we got from there to here in drug control

It shocks most Americans to learn that opium, morphine, cocaine, heroin, and marijuana were legally sold without Federal controls from the early days of this nation until 1915. As these drugs were introduced to the American marketplace, they could be bought from pharmacies, grocery stores, doctors, peddlers, and eventually by mail order from retailers such as Sears Roebuck. There were no Federal restrictions even on sales to minors. Only a few states made any attempt to control drug marketing. Most of these products were vigorously advertised and promoted the same as other pharmaceutical or recreational substances. Patent medicine manufacturers sold medications containing heavy portions of these drugs without any effort to disclose their contents to the consumer. America has had a long history with legal narcotics, cocaine, sedatives, stimulants, and hypnotics.

With such a laissez-faire attitude toward addictive psychoactive drugs, was America a nation of drug junkies in the 19th century and the early decades of this century? To know our enemy in the drug war is to know ourselves. In this chapter we will look back to that time when all drugs were legal to see how and why the United States prohibited narcotics and cocaine. Then we will compare that experience with the prohibition of alcohol. Finally, let us determine how America's drug and crime problem got out of control and why the United States declared War on Drugs in 1972.

Recreational use of psychoactive drugs, other than alcohol, was not common among the early settlers in North America. Alcoholic beverages were brought from Europe; nicotine (tobacco) was adopted from the American Indians; and caffeine (coffee and tea) was imported from Asia by traders. Coca leaves were known in the Spanish colonies of South America but were not introduced in the English colonies. Marijuana, too, remained in the Spanish domain. Another form of cannabis, hemp, was grown in the English colonies for use in cordage, not in drugs. Hemp plants and opium poppies had been taken from Asia to Europe and thence to North America. The dried juice of an unripe opium seed pod was sometimes dissolved in alcoholic beverages, or taken in some way that diluted the impact of the active agent. A tincture of opium in the form of laudanum, containing alcohol, or black drop, containing no alcohol, were familiar resources for pain relief. Benjamin Franklin regularly used laudanum in his later life to relieve the pain of kidney stones.[1] But opium never became a recreational substance like tobacco, tea, or coffee, and the recreational drug of choice among the early settlers was certainly alcohol.

Developments in organic chemistry in the 1800s changed the available forms of drugs derived from opium poppies and the coca shrub. The opiate called morphine was isolated in the first decade, and cocaine was extracted from the coca leaves in 1844. In 1874, diacetylmorphine (heroin) was synthesized from morphine. By mid-century the hypodermic syringe was perfected, and had become a familiar instrument to American physicians and patients by 1870. The astounding growth of the pharmaceutical industry during this period intensified the impact of narcotics and cocaine upon the American society. As the century wore on, manufacturers grew increasingly adept at exploiting a marketable innovation and moving it into mass production.[2]

The potential danger of opium addiction had been recognized long before the availability of morphine and the hypodermic syringe. The American Dispensatory of 1818 noted that the habitual use of opium could lead to "tremors, paralysis, stupidity and general emaciation." The same report also proclaimed the extraordinary value of opium in a multitude of ailments ranging from cholera to asthma. Considering the treatments then in vogue—blistering, vomiting, and bleeding—we can understand why opium was as cherished by patients as by their physicians.[3]

The expanding market for opium, opiates, coca, and cocaine in 19th-century America, occurred during an era of wide availability and unrestrained advertising. The powerful new forms of opium and cocaine were more readily available in America than in most nations. Under the U.S. Constitution, individual states assumed responsibility for health issues. The lack of uniformity in state laws, as well as the absence of any Federal control, created a relaxed atmosphere for drug manufacturers. Contrasted with the American experience, a central authority in European nations usually exercised a greater control over a physician's right to practice and the availability of dangerous drugs.[4]

The Enemy Is Us

Opium use for other than medicinal purposes came to this country with the Chinese immigrants in the middle 19th century, and was restricted mainly to that community until the importation of smoking opium was outlawed in 1909. After the Civil War this country experienced a growing drug addiction problem. Morphine, a derivative of opium, introduced to the world by Frederick W. A. Serturner in 1803, came to be valued by physicians as a most effective pain-killer. Its liberal and prolonged use by doctors in the Civil War to ease the pain of the wounded is generally believed to have caused many of the veterans to become addicted. However, according to Yale University medical historian Dr. David Musto, recent studies reveal that morphine was usually dusted or rubbed into wounds, and only sometimes injected.[5] Morphine addiction during the late 19th century was often referred to as the soldier's disease, although it was never established how widespread was addiction among the veteran population.

Cocaine became the miracle drug of the 1880s. Dr. Carl Koller, an Austrian ophthalmologic surgeon, first used it medically in 1884. It quickly gained wide acceptance as a local anesthetic, because of its effectiveness in depressing nerve endings without damaging the sensitive tissue of the nose, throat, and cornea. One of America's most prominent neurologists, William A. Hammond, extolled cocaine in print and lectures. By 1887, Hammond was assuring audiences that cocaine was no more habit-forming than coffee or tea.[6] Sigmund Freud became one of Europe's leading advocate of cocaine and wrote extensively of its benefits in psychoanalysis. Freud lost his enthusiasm for the drug a few years later, when he watched his good friend Von Fleishl die from a nervous disorder exacerbated by cocaine addiction, while he stood by, helplessly.[7]

In the late 19th century, the smoking of hashish and the eating of hashish candy became fashionable among a few members of the "idle rich." (Hashish is derived from hemp, a cannabis plant related to marijuana.) The smoking of marijuana became popular in the 1920s in "artistic" enclaves like New York's Greenwich Village and New Orleans' French Quarter. Some farm workers were reported to smoke "grass" early in the 20th century, while a few soldiers brought back the practice from the Mexican border in 1915 and a few sailors from Mexican ports in the 1920s. But for these exceptions, marijuana use was of little consequence during this period, or even in 1937, when it was added to the list of prohibited substances.[8]

Knowing the Enemy

Meanwhile, in the United States, patent medicines were gaining wide acceptance and were sold over the counter, without regulation. Most of these concoctions were liberally laced with alcohol, opium, cocaine, heroin, or marijuana and were frequently sold as "cure-alls." Many of America's finest ladies and gentlemen would swear by their "medicine" as the thing that kept them going, without any idea of the contents of that mixture. The marketplace operated under a policy of "Buyer beware," and laws demanding labeling of contents were years away.

A proliferation of other products flooded the market. Among them were McMunn's Elixir of Opium and Globe of Flower Cough Syrup. Vin Mariani, the original French Coca Wine, had a devoted following including the likes of Ulysses Grant, Thomas Edison, and Pope Leo XIII. Full-page advertisements in popular periodicals of the day, such as Harper's Weekly, bragged of an album containing no fewer than 600 endorsements "of persons of distinction in the world of Authors, Composers, Physicians, Lawyers, Churchmen, Painters, Lyric and Dramatic Artists, Statesmen, Journalists, and Poets, who have, as if by mutual collaboration, extended appropriate words of praise for services rendered to each individually for the beneficial results obtained from the use of this famous wine, a la coca, bearing Monsieur Mariani's name."[9]

This particular advertisement, of October 28, 1893, contains the portraits and endorsements of seven world-prominent personalities and, in part, concludes by saying:

> Briefly stated, "Vin Mariani" is a perfectly safe and reliable diffusible stimulant and tonic; a powerful aid to digestion and assimilation; admirably adapted for children, invalids, and convalescents. It improves the appetite, and also has a remarkable effect in strengthening the voice and in maintaining its tone. For these purposes it is largely employed by clergymen, actors, et live genus omne who are called on to speak in public.[10]

There are many examples of the drug and beverage industries aggressively advertising and marketing the opiates and cocaine without full knowledge or warning of their danger. The Parke-Davis Company provided coca and cocaine in 15 forms, and proudly advertised that the drug, "can supply the place of food, make the coward brave, the silent eloquent and...render the sufferer insensitive to pain."[11] Parke-Davis also rolled cocaine into cigars, and advertised them to the public to "cure the blues." The Coca Cola company sold its popular drink from 1885 to 1903, before it removed cocaine from the original formula, replacing it with caffeine. In 1898, the Bayer Company introduced its new miracle drug with the trade name "Heroin" and advertised it as a remedy for many ailments. Ironically, it was initially offered as a cure for morphine addiction.[12]

As consumption of opiates and cocaine increased during the 19th century, so did the frequency of addiction. Opium or cocaine addiction brought shame whatever the cause—over-prescribing by physicians, excessive use of over-the-counter medicines, self-indulgence, or "weak will." In the last decade of the 19th century, there was a growing realization that many Americans were unwittingly becoming addicted to medications containing large portions of narcotics that were undisclosed to the consumer. Much blame also fell on the medical profession for irresponsibility in prescribing narcotics over long periods, without considering the consequence of addiction. Medical societies were successfully pressured to reform prescription practices. Public concern led to passage of the Pure Food and Drug Act in 1906, with its labeling rules. Consequently, the decline in the use of psychoactive drugs after 1896 was related mostly to the public's growing fear of addiction and the rising social intolerance to the casual use of habit-forming substances.[13]

If there is such a thing as a drug addict's paradise, it was the United States at the beginning of this century. Drugs were cheap, available, and legal. However, drug addiction had already begun to decrease as a result of education of the public, society's growing intolerance of recreational drug use, and, after 1906, federal labeling laws. In spite of the availability of cheap drugs sold over the counter to anyone by local merchants, there was no big crime problem associated with, or caused by, the use of these drugs. Drug abusers and drug addicts were treated by their personal physicians, or in public health clinics, as any other patients would be treated. Drug addiction was subject to social ostracism, but was still considered a medical problem. Yet, in spite of this laissez-faire attitude toward drug control, America, by all historical accounts, was largely a moral, vibrant, hard-working, and prosperous society. The United States had many social problems, including relatively high—though declining—rates of alcoholism and other addictions. But it was certainly not a nation of drug junkies.

Knowing the Enemy

The end to unrestricted drug use

A great moral reform was sweeping over the United States in the late 1890s that would continue until after World War I. The temperance movement was gaining momentum at the turn of the century, and social concern over drunkenness spilled over to the problem of drug addiction. Drug habitués were few in number compared to drunkards and only constituted a quarter of one percent of that population. But social intolerance of "dope fiends" had reached a point where there were no political defenders of recreational drug use by the second decade of this century.

Excessive drinking of alcohol had been a problem in the United States since its founding, especially because of its damage to family life. In 1784, Dr. Benjamin Rush, signer of the Declaration of Independence and "father of psychiatry," published a book urging temperance but not total abstinence. In the same year both the Quakers and the Methodists urged their members to abstain from hard liquor. Meanwhile, "the period from the 1790s to the early 1830s was probably the heaviest drinking era in the nation's history."[14] The first local temperance society was founded in Moreau, New York, in 1808, and the American Temperance Society was founded in 1826. For almost a century there was a contest between the forces of temperance and those of abstinence ("teetotalism"). Increasingly the teetotalers moved toward prohibition. Prohibition laws were passed in a dozen states between 1851 and 1855. Then, as slavery became the chief national issue, prohibition laws were repealed or left unenforced. Although estimated per capita consumption of alcohol had fallen from a high of 7.10 gallons per year in 1830 to 2.07 gallons in 1870, many people—especially women—were not satisfied. The Woman's Christian Temperance Union (WCTU) was founded in 1874. The WCTU and its allies were "now more willing than ever before to impose their views on society for its own good" in the words of two authorities, Mark Edward Lender and James Kirby Martin. Prohibitionists' zeal was not dampened by the fact that consumption of alcohol kept falling. Panic about "Demon Rum" was fed by the flood of European immigrants with their traditions of social drinking. Yet Professors Lender and Martin conclude that "the new immigrants did not generally contribute to national alcohol problems."[15]

During the so called Progressive Era (1899-1916) "many reformers...were eager to prohibit drinking entirely."[16] Leading

17

physicians and industrialists, including Rockefeller and Ford, got on the prohibitionist bandwagon. The Anti-Saloon League offered support to both Democratic and Republican candidates pledged to prohibition. So many "Drys" were elected to the House and Senate in 1916 that the 18th Amendment, prohibiting "the manufacture, sale, or transportation of intoxicating liquors," passed easily in 1917. Meanwhile a wartime act prohibited the conversion of grains into beverages. The 18th Amendment was ratified by the states by 1919, to go into effect a year later. The enabling Volstead Act, passed over President Wilson's veto, set up the prohibitionist framework as of January 1920.

Although the addicting nature of tobacco was reported as early as 1527 by Bishop de las Casas, there have been few laws prohibiting the sale of nicotine-containing products except to minors. Oddly 14 states passed and repealed laws prohibiting cigarettes in the 1920s. Of course smoking usually has been prohibited in certain places for reason of health and public safety. Many private studies have warned against the dangers of tobacco—smoked, chewed, or inhaled—and in 1964 the U.S. Surgeon General warned that smoking shortens life. In that same year Congress passed a law requiring health warnings on cigarette packages. Education, however, remains the chief weapon against nicotine. Education, moreover, has always been the only weapon against over-consumption of caffeine in tea, coffee, or cola drinks. Education also is the chief weapon against the misuse of inhalants: both anesthetics such as ether and a wide range of household products including gasoline, glues, and paint removers.[17]

Unlike today's drug problem, much drug use before 1906 began without the user of medications realizing the presence of narcotics or cocaine. Once made aware by labels that their patent medicines contained heavy portions of addicting drugs, most people were able and willing to put the preparations aside and clear their medicine shelves of the offending products. Those who had developed a dependency problem often were treated by their physicians to wean them from the offending drug. Drug habitués were not isolated from society as criminals, as they are today, and many continued to function reasonably well in society, while under the care of their physicians. To stop indiscriminate use of alcohol, narcotics, and cocaine in medicines, Congress passed the Pure Food and Drug Act in 1906, as noted before, requiring descriptive labels. This was the first action by the federal government in addressing the domestic drug problem of the nation.

Spurred on by the zeal of the alcohol prohibition movement, some reformers called on government to assume the moral responsibility for freeing the "lower classes" and the "weak-willed" from the temptations of drugs.

The federal government prohibited the importation of opium for smoking into the United States, in 1909, yet left other opiates legal. Ironically, this legislation had little to do with the domestic control of narcotics, since opium for smoking primarily affected only a small number of immigrant Chinese. It was hurriedly passed for the benefit of the State Department, so the American delegation at the International Opium Commission in Shanghai could say that the United States had opium control legislation. To be sure, missionaries had expressed concern about the opium trade in China and in the new U.S. colony, the Philippines. Also between 1875 and 1914 twenty-seven U.S. states and cities outlawed opium smoking.[18]

The Harrison Narcotics Act was passed on December 17, 1914, at the insistence of the State Department, to demonstrate the United States' commitment to worldwide narcotics control. It became effective on the first day of March, 1915. Dr. Hamilton Wright, the State Department's Opium Commissioner, had been embarrassed while attending the International Conference on Opium at the Hague in December 1911. The German delegation asked for assurance that the United States would enact implementing legislation to enforce an international treaty should Germany sign and ratify it. Dr. Wright and the State Department were more interested in improving their negotiating position in the International Conference on Opium than in controlling domestic uses of narcotics. There were many misgivings in Congress about this legislation, but its passage was urgent to prevent embarrassment to President Wilson and the State Department in their newly found prominence on the international scene.[19]

The Harrison Act made it illegal to obtain pure narcotics and cocaine without a prescription. It also limited the amounts of narcotics contained in patent medicines. Cocaine was banned from use in these medicines. After passage of the Act, most addicts were legally maintained on drugs by prescription through their physicians. Dr. Wright and the Internal Revenue Service, which was charged with the responsibility of enforcement, argued that the Harrison Act forbade indefinite maintenance of addiction unless there was a specific medical reason such as cancer or tuberculosis[20]. Since addiction was not generally considered a disease, the argument went, an addict was not a patient. Many physicians were arrested under the IRS interpretation. That interpretation, however, was rejected by the U.S. Supreme Court in 1916.

The on-rushing alcohol temperance movement, resulting in the passage of alcohol prohibition, hardened the position of majorities in both political parties against the ravages of drug addiction. In this climate, the Supreme Court reversed itself by a 5-4 vote in 1919 and made the prohibition of narcotics absolute. The justices ruled that maintaining addicts on narcotic drugs, even by a doctor's prescription, was not good faith practice of medicine. By coincidence, the prohibition of alcohol and the prohibition of narcotics and cocaine became effective the same month, January 1920. While alcohol prohibition was achieved by Constitutional amendment, narcotics and cocaine were prohibited by Congressional legislation buttressed by a Supreme Court interpretation of the Harrison Narcotics Act. Within a year, drug clinics in about 70 cities closed. Marijuana was outlawed in 46 of the 48 states between 1927 and 1937; in the latter year Congress banned it nationally except for restricted medicinal use.[21]

The noble experiment begins.

In 1920, the "Noble Experiment," as President Hoover called it, was under way. Alcohol and drug use ceased to be a medical problem, and was now a law-enforcement problem. Prohibition did not altogether deter America from its drinking habits, and the law met with widespread opposition. Bootlegging, speakeasies, hip flasks, and rum-running became familiar terms in the public consciousness.

The weight of historical evidence shows that prohibition brought significant drops in consumption of alcohol, arrests for drunkenness, and deaths from alcoholic diseases. But the Noble Experiment carried a heavy price. Part of that price—which is difficult to quantify—was the widespread cynicism about the law, since so many citizens broke the law to evade prohibition. This cynicism was especially worrisome when it affected the younger generation, resulting in the Twenties' "flaming youth" who took delight in flouting the law. But the greater price, evident to all, was the explosion of organized crime. The consensus of historians is that "the immediate occasion of the rise of gangs was undoubtedly prohibition."[22]

Knowing the Enemy

The greatest beneficiaries of prohibition were the underworld elements, who imported, manufactured, and sold alcohol and drugs outside the law. Gangsters dominated the "roaring Twenties." Al Capone, the mobster who controlled the beer and liquor trade in the Chicago area, and his counterparts in other major U.S. cities, seemed to be above the law. Usually they were, since they had bought the cooperation of many law enforcement officials. They controlled the alcohol distribution in every major city of the USA Bloated with the fantastic profits created by prohibition, organized crime on a national scale became a reality during that period.

The Mafia accepted the opportunity presented to them, courtesy of our government, and filled the void created when legitimate businesses had to withdraw from the narcotics and alcohol trades. One of the more powerful Mafia bosses, Salvatore Lucania ("Lucky Luciano"), convinced the "family" bosses across the nation that it would be to their mutual benefit to cooperate rather than fight with each other, and in 1931 organized "The Commission." This loose federation of Mafia chieftains made decisions for all the "families" and the Mafia grew rich and powerful from the lucrative profits of illegal alcohol.[23]

The use of illegal drugs and alcohol became difficult to estimate after prohibition in 1920, with both enterprises operating underground. Thirty thousand physicians were arrested during the 1920s for dispensing narcotics, and some 3,000 actually served prison sentences. Because of the government's hard line, drug clinics, including state-operated clinics, were closed down during the 1920s, and doctors abandoned the treatment of addicts in the United States for nearly half a century.

Narcotic agents numbered about one-tenth of the dry agents, and narcotics violations were fewer than Volstead violations during the 1920s. Yet almost a third of federal prisoners were Harrison Act violators, because of the severity of judges and juries. This number was more than the combined total of the next two categories—liquor violations and car theft.[24] The wardens of the Atlanta and Leavenworth penitentiaries urged for many years the creation of special prisons for drug addicts, since prisons were not equipped to care for addicts and their association with other prisoners was bad for both groups. The Narcotic Farm bill finally became law in 1929, but the Lexington, Kentucky, farm was not opened until 1935 and the Fort Worth, Texas, farm until 1938. Moreover, addicts at the farms were treated more like convicts than patients. As Dr. Musto writes: "The conditions under which the psychiatrists worked helps explain their disenchantment with the Federal Bureau of Narcotics and the 'legal approach' toward addiction. Not until the late 1960s were the bars removed from the Lexington facility and the cells turned into rooms. These farms had been exactly what the wardens envisioned in the mid-1920s—additional prison space for convicted addicts."[25]

Evaluating the drug menace during this period depended upon whom you chose to believe: a crusader such as Richmond P. Hobson, Spanish American War hero, former congressman, and prohibition propagandist, or U.S. Public Health Service officials, Lawrence Kolb, Sr. and Andrew Grover DuMez. A report issued by Kolb and DuMez in 1924 stated that there were probably only 110,000 addicts in the nation. This report was met by a strong rebuttal from Hobson, who believed that narcotics, particularly heroin, prompted crime and drove users to commit the most horrible acts. Hobson's impact on drug policy-making is summarized by Yale's Dr. Musto:

> Organizations like the White Cross [International Anti-Narcotics Society], which had members at least as sincere and seem to have had more direct contact with the addict than the Hobson organizations had, were fought because they tried to reestablish maintenance, a once respectable mode of care but one which would have wrecked the prohibitive enforcement law on which federal narcotic controls were based. Overall, the propaganda spread by zealots like Hobson was accepted as true, and addicts were perceived as an immense evil which should be blotted out of society.[26]

The Journal of the American Medical Association (JAMA) complained of Hobson's distortions and exaggerations. Levi G. Nutt, head of the Narcotics Division, "thought there were fewer addicts than the Kolb and DuMez estimate, but the Hobson associations kept on fighting, spreading fear and producing statements that were faithfully repeated by other national organizations, fraternal orders, and radio networks; all felt that by relaying Hobson's message that they were serving their nation."[27] In a 1928 national radio broadcast over NBC, Hobson declared that "upon the issue [of drug addiction] hangs the perpetuation of civilization, the destiny of the world and the future of the human race."[28] That is a rather ominous and ridiculous accusation to hang on a few harmful substances—particularly on opium, a drug that has been available to mankind for most of recorded history.

Hobson did stumble upon one truth in a 1929 radio broadcast when he stated: "Ten years ago the narcotic drug addiction problem in America was a minor, medical problem. Today it is a major, national problem, constituting the chief factor menacing the public health, the public morals, the public safety."[29] He was trying to point up the menace of spreading drug addiction, but inadvertently acknowledged that after drug prohibition a minor medical problem with drug addiction turned into a major, wide-sweeping drug dilemma that was menacing America's public health, morals, and safety. Drug prohibition, not drug addiction, remains a national problem sixty-five years later, while the repeal of alcohol prohibition reduced alcohol-related problems to manageable proportions.

Although Hobson was not respected by hard-liners within the federal bureaucracy like Harry Anslinger, the crusader's propaganda helped the prohibitionist cause. Anslinger became head of the Federal Bureau of Narcotics, within the Treasury Department, in 1932, and was given responsibility for enforcing the anti-drug laws. Anslinger was a powerful figure in that position and was influential in having the 1937 law passed to prohibit the use of marijuana. He was successful in thwarting all attempts to classify drug addicts as people needing medical help. Although adamantly opposed to the administering of prohibited drugs even for medical purposes, he did accept establishment of the aforementioned hospitals at Lexington and Fort Worth where addicts could go, or would forcibly be sent, for detoxification.

Prohibition fails.

The prohibition of alcohol was coming under increasing attack in the early 1930s, by its opponents, known as the "Wets." They made three charges against prohibition: that it was ineffective in curbing drinking, that it represented an unnecessary restriction on personal choice, and that it created crime and public corruption. The Wets' charges resulted in a successful campaign to repeal the 18th Amendment. Although the "Dry" Herbert Hoover had trounced the Wet Al Smith in 1928, Franklin D. Roosevelt was elected on a Wet platform in 1932. In 1933, the 18th Amendment was repealed and legitimate private enterprises once again became the manufacturers and sellers of alcoholic beverages.

Unfortunately, federal leadership did not recognize the parallel between prohibition of alcohol and the prohibition of drugs. The drug users were few in number, and there was little public tolerance for the dope addict. Although marijuana use was limited and presented no particular problem, it became a target of the Narcotics Bureau. Commissioner Anslinger's office released dramatic and exaggerated portrayals of marijuana's effects. Scientific publications during the 1930s also fearfully described marijuana's dangers. The federal government's lack of candor about marijuana would come back to haunt the narcotics enforcement authorities. Marijuana is now known to present health hazards, like tobacco, but not to create monstrous criminals as in Stevenson's "Dr. Jekyll and Mr. Hyde." Exaggeration fell in the face of the realities of drug use, which led to a loss of credibility regarding any government pronouncement on drugs.[30]

The Mafia organizes the illegal drug trade.

Organized crime lost its primary source of funds with the repeal of alcohol prohibition; however, the illegal drug trade offered other opportunities. In spite of the draconian policies of Harry Anslinger, Americans continued to use drugs, although the use was confined mostly to the larger urban areas. The Mafia was in a position, with its worldwide organization, to exploit the illegal drug trade. Boss Luciano directed the importation of heroin and set up the distribution system within the United States. He was the major player in this smuggling operation, remaining active even after his deportation in the 1950s and up until his death in Italy in 1962.

Drug use began to slowly increase after World War II when the Mafia was able to reestablish its overseas connections. Still drug use remained out of the mainstream of society, being relegated primarily to the slums, and to groups such as jazz musicians. Recreational use of drugs was confined pretty much to heroin, while the use of other drugs, such as marijuana, cocaine, and synthetic stimulants, hallucinogens, and sedatives, which are used so frequently today, remained at a fairly low level during the 1950s. It was the emergence of the "beat" generation that pushed drug use into the consciousness of the nation. The "beats"-- also called "beatniks"—were the rebels against conformity and middle class values. Drug use was the symbol of their intellectual and moral alienation from society. Although few in numbers, the beatniks were an influence on the nation's disenchanted.

Knowing the Enemy

The stormy Sixties and increasing drug use.

The 1960s was a watershed decade in many respects, including the changes in drug use. The changing drug scene is described by sociologist Erich Goode:

"A vigorous drug subculture came into existence. During this time some social groups viewed drug use in positive terms, evaluated individuals on the basis of whether or not they used illegal drugs, and believed it a virtue to 'turn on' someone who did not use drugs. This subculture was a powerful force in recruiting young people into the use of illegal psychoactive drugs."[31]

This author's observation is that changes in attitudes and behavior preceded the explosive increase in the use of psychoactive drugs. These changes took place in a postwar social environment, The historian Frederick Lewis Allen has given a cogent description of such a society: "After a war in which the national will is focused on an agreed-upon goal, people are likely to be tired, irritable, disputatious, prone to let their responsibilities go,...and prone to indulge in feverish activities."[32] Because the start of the Cold War and the Korean War came on the heels of World War II, the start of America's postwar era was delayed until 1954. It continued until 1964, when the Gulf of Tonkin incident marked the beginning of a larger war in Vietnam. When people let their responsibilities go, they reject their traditional values. Illegal drug use is the manifestation of the rejection of accepted social values of America's mainstream. You cannot blame any one person or institution for the rise of the drug subculture as a corruptive influence in our society, but there were some large contributors.

One bad influence was the "jet set": over-privileged individuals from bigtime sport, entertainment, and inherited wealth. The jet set glamorized over-indulgence in all formally taboo activities, including the use of drugs, especially cocaine. Playboy magazine probably did more than the contraceptive "pill" to promote sexual promiscuity. Hugh Hefner, editor and founder of Playboy, espoused an unconventional attitude toward family, government, and religion on its pages. He encouraged non-conformist writers to criticize traditional values and the moral laws of the land. The old immorality of past societies was wrapped in a new package, decorated with enticing pictures of nude young women, and offered to an impressionable youthful audience as the new morality for modern America. Marijuana was glorified, and readers were advised as to which States had lax laws or lax enforcement against its use. The popularity of Playboy allowed it to attract prominent mainstream writers, and the magazine presented an aura of authenticity for its counterculture philosophies. Playboy's success brought on many imitators, but none achieved the avant-garde position in the subculture that Playboy enjoyed.

"Turn on, tune in, drop out."

The late Timothy Leary, originally a respectable psychologist, became the "guru" of hallucinogenic drugs. Natural hallucinogens—peyote cactus, certain mushrooms, and other plants—were used in a limited way by some Indians. In the years 1938-43, LSD was synthesized. Leary became the most vocal and public advocate of LSD. Like a Pied Piper, he led a host of disaffected young people down a destructive path with the rallying cry of "Turn on, tune in, drop out." Aldous Huxley, the author, and many others joined Dr. Leary in encouraging Americans to experience the consciousness expansion and mind opening effects of LSD. While LSD was all the rage in the drug subculture, it soon earned a bad reputation from the fatalities associated with hallucinations. Earlier in the 1950s, a hush-hush CIA experiment to give LSD to unwitting subjects resulted in the reported loss of a senior officer, who felt he was losing his mind and jumped out of a high-rise hotel window. This was followed by many other publicized instances of "bad trips" that resulted in death. Then there was the problem with unpredictable "flash-backs"--a recurrence of hallucinations when no new dose has been taken. It was these "flash-backs" that were of particular concern to the Armed Forces. The author viewed a Navy training film in the late 1960s advising servicemen that the chemical changes in the brain after taking LSD approximate the brain chemistry of a psychotic. In essence, LSD induces temporarily insanity in a person. In 1968, the government banned LSD, and the Armed Forces prohibited its use for military personnel.[33]

While many leading Americans questioned the U.S. involvement in Vietnam, President Johnson's sending of 125,000 troops in 1965 aroused the opposition of a large part of the public. The Vietnam War gave the anti-establishment forces a rallying cause and a reason to question every government action. The use and sale of all kinds of illegal drugs skyrocketed, and psychoactive drug use became socially acceptable for a large segment of our society. The "hippies," the name applied to that group of our young people that had dropped out of society and congregated in sections of our larger cities, popularized the smoking of marijuana, which, along with their non-conformist dress, could be considered their trademark. The popular notion that marijuana use would lead to use of more potent drugs seemed confirmed when heroin use soared among the "hippies" in places like Haight-Ashbury section of San Francisco[34]. On the other hand, Commissioner Anslinger himself testified in 1937 that he had never heard of a case where marijuana use led to use of hard drugs. Moreover, the injection of "speed" (amphetamines) increased in San Francisco in 1967 after police cracked down on sources of marijuana and LSD.[35]

The drug war begins.

The rapid spread of illicit drug use in the stormy Sixties led President Nixon to declare a War on Drugs in 1972. To put the problem in perspective, the reader should note that drug abuse occurred among a small minority of Americans. Alarm was caused by the rate of growth of this minority of abusers. That increase had happened despite the series of drug control laws starting in 1914. Congress, urged by the President, met the problem with a broader and tighter law, the Comprehensive Drug Abuse and Prevention Act of 1970. Most states passsed similar laws.

The 1970 Act distinguished "among several categories of drugs based on their abuse potential and their medical utility." One category consisted of drugs considered to have a high potential for abuse and no presently accepted medical use (including heroin, LSD and the other halucinogens, and marijuana). These became prohibited except in federally approved research. A second category consisted of drugs considered to have a high abuse potential along with some accepted medical use (including morphine, cocaine, methaqualone, amphetamines, and short-acting barbiturates). These became controlled by rigid prescription procedures. A third category consisted of drugs supposed to have a lower abuse potential plus accepted medical use (including non-narcotic painkillers, long-acting barbiturates, and tranquilizers such as Valium). These were to have less rigid controls.

The Enemy Is Us

The Comprehensive Drug Abuse and Prevention Act of 1970 is considered as the beginning of the War on Drugs by Erich Goode and the effect of the first 16 years of that war is described by Goode:

> The demand for drugs for illegal purposes remains high in spite of law-enforcement efforts. For example, between 1970 and 1977, the number of arrests on marijuana charges in the United States more than doubled, from 188,000 to 457,000. During this same period, however, the percentage of the American population who had ever used marijuana also doubled for most age categories. Arrest did not seem to deter marijuana use. Likewise, the number of arrests on the charge of narcotics possession and sale increased from 533,000 in 1980 to over 850,000 in 1988. Yet the use of heroin and the other narcotics held its own during this period, while the use of cocaine exploded. Nonetheless, in the face of mounting public concern, Congress passed strong new drug laws and enforcement measures, along with treatment and education programs, in 1986.[36]

These strong new drug laws, passed in 1986, have been in effect for a decade—sufficient time to see significant changes, if any are to be forthcoming. The results from the drug war have to be disappointing to all—from the agents in the front lines to the White House, to the members of Congress, and especially to the American public. All had hoped for more from the amount of money and effort expended on this War on Drugs. It's a step forward here and a step back there. The U.S.A. essentially is marking time at a level of very high drug use.

3

BUGLER, SOUND RETREAT
A retreat from a wrong direction is the
only wise move in the right direction.

The United States government's first attempt to control addictive drugs came after the 1898 acquisition of the Philippine Islands. Smoking opium by the indigenous population in that new U.S. colony was a fairly widespread practice. American officials and influential clergymen considered it the government's moral duty to discourage the use of opium by our newly acquired dependents. Our government also feared that American servicemen stationed in the islands might fall prey to the habit. The United States colonial administration hoped to avoid China's problem of societal malaise that resulted in great part from opium smoking. The specter of the Chinese drug addiction problem, as well as the subsequent Boxer Rebellion to break free of China's subjugation to Western powers, was fresh in the mind of Theodore Roosevelt Administration officials.

When Spain controlled the Philippines, opium use was permitted. However, the island's Spanish governor maintained an opium monopoly that required opium traders to buy the drug from the colonial government. William Howard Taft, the newly appointed U.S. Governor General of the Philippines, suggested the continuation of the monopoly and proposed to use the revenue from sales in a massive education program for the new Philippine dependents. In this way, he hoped to discourage the use of opium through education and pay for the program with opium profits, thereby avoiding a costly alternative program.

An aggressive move in the wrong direction

President Theodore Roosevelt rejected Taft's proposal. In 1905, Congress mandated an outright prohibition of opium in the Philippines for any purpose other than medical. Although a paragon of rugged individualism, Roosevelt ignored one of his maxims: An individual is

29

responsible for his actions. He rejected individual responsibility and substituted a government edict to control personal behavior. Up to this time the federal government had allowed any personal practice as long as it did not clearly and directly injure others. There was no dispute that widespread addiction had a social consequence. However, the social cost of prohibition had never been calculated. The possibility that prohibition would come with a high price tag was not a consideration in the Roosevelt Administration's decision. The decision to <u>prohibit</u> opium use in the Philippines later led the State Department to lobby Congress for domestic drug control legislation to support the international opium control treaty.

A great moral reformation was sweeping the United States at the turn of the century. The spirit of reform was manifest in the paternal attitude of government officials, who were eager to lift every citizen to a higher plateau of morality. The teetotalers in the temperance movement who spearheaded the reformation deemed it the moral duty of our government to remove the temptation of alcohol and drugs from the weak-willed or those lacking in character. The Protestant Episcopal bishop of the Philippines, Charles Henry Brent, was a close friend of Governor General Taft, and epitomized the moral responsibility of those in authority. He was to play a key role in the United States' initial efforts at drug control.

Society's attitude had hardened against drunkards and drug habitués toward the end of the 19th century—a change similar to the attitude of today's society toward tobacco smokers. By the first decade of the 20th century there was growing support in Congress and from the public to regulate narcotics to prevent addiction, <u>but there was little support for an outright ban of any drug</u>. The temperance movement wanted alcohol banned entirely, and addictive drugs were pulled into the reform by the fervor of the campaign. The simplest and most direct way to stop substance abuse, according to those in the movement, was to prohibit the manufacture, importation, sale, or transportation of abused substances in or out of the United States. A leading authority, David F. Musto, describes the mood: "Prohibitionists believed that their reform could be made to work, perhaps not perfectly but well enough to rid this nation of such glaring evils as the saloon. The movement was supported by the characteristic Progressive assumption that government could change or neutralize the habits of large groups by well written legislation and honest enforcement."[1] Prohibition was to be The Noble Experiment.

The prohibition of opium in the Philippines was the initial move in the wrong direction for drug control, since it attempted to prevent foolish or unwise behavior with police action. In hind-sight, Taft's proposal to influence personal health and habits with persuasion and education was a better alternative, although private enterprise would have been preferred to a government-operated opium monopoly. With prohibition the government had created the additional problems of controlling opium smuggling and policing those individuals who defied the smoking ban. This was to be a larger problem than anticipated.

The second move in the wrong direction.

The second error came with the strategy chosen to enforce the opium ban in the Philippine Islands. Roosevelt administration officials held the popular belief that controlling crops and traffic in drug-producing countries could dry up the supply and most efficiently stop consumption of drugs for nonmedical use in U.S. possessions.[2] The Administration's choice of strategy led, step-by-step, directly to the enactment of the 1914 Harrison Narcotics Act, and ultimately mired this nation in a major drug control morass where we are stuck to this day. Roosevelt had employed "gunboat diplomacy" on occasions in Colombia, the Dominican Republic, and Venezuela, and was not hesitant to lean on foreign counties to obtain their cooperation. It is not surprising that his administration favored this strategy. Unfortunately, it forced the United States to rely upon other governments and foreign individuals to act in our interest. Most often, drug control for America's benefit is contrary to the economic interests or concerns of drug-producing nations.

The control of opium crops and drug trafficking in source countries required the cooperation of regional interests, so the U.S. convened an Opium Commission of regional powers in Shanghai in 1909. As Professor Musto reports, "The Protestant Episcopal bishop of the Philippines, Charles Henry Brent, who had been instrumental in organizing the meeting, was chosen to preside. Resolutions noting problems with opium and opiates were adopted, but they did not constitute a treaty, and no decisions bound the nations attending the commission. In diplomatic parlance, what was needed now was a conference not a commission. The U.S. began to pursue that goal with determination."[3]

The Enemy Is Us

The China Factor.

The opium trade in the 19th century was highly profitable to western nations and particularly to the British. China attempted to deal with the problem of addiction from smoking opium by restricting its cultivation and importation. The British objected, and the resulting dispute led to the First Opium War between Britain and China in 1839-42. The loss of that war forced the Chinese to open five ports to British merchants, cede Hong Kong to Britain, and grant Britain the right to try British citizens residing in China. Other western powers were soon granted similar privileges, ending China's long isolation from other civilizations. China's Second Opium War (1856-60), with the British and French, also arose from China's objection to the opium trade and resulted in another humiliating defeat for the Chinese. China agreed to the Treaty of Tianjin, which opened 11 more ports. It also allowed foreign envoys to reside in Beijing; admitted missionaries to China; permitted foreigners to travel in the Chinese interior; and legalized the importation of opium.[4]

The Boxer Uprising in China (1898-1900) was coincident with the United States' acquisition of the Philippine Islands and America's growing involvement in Asia. This was a violent movement by the Chinese people to rid their country of foreigners and foreign influences. The Boxers (from the name of their movement, "righteous harmony fists") rampaged throughout China, killing foreigners as well as Christian Chinese and other Chinese with ties to foreigners. An international force of British, French, German, Japanese, Russian, and U.S. troops entered Beijing in August 1900 to lift the siege of the foreign legations there. Under the subsequent protocol of September 1901, China was forced to pay an indemnity and to yield to several new foreign demands—notably the right to station troops at the legations in Beijing and along the route to the sea.[5]

By understanding China's humiliation at the hands of the western nations, one can appreciate the significance the China factor played in the development of the United States' drug strategy. This point is brought into focus by David F. Musto, psychiatrist and professor of medical history at Yale:

> In early 1906 China had instituted a campaign against opium, especially smoking opium, in an attempt to modernize and to

32

make the Empire better able to cope with continued Western encroachments on its sovereignty. At about the same time, Chinese anger at maltreatment of their nationals in the U.S. seethed into a voluntary boycott of American goods. Partly to appease the Chinese by aiding their anti opium efforts and partly to deal with uncontrollable smuggling within the Philippine Archipelago, the U.S. convened a meeting of regional powers. In this way, the U.S. launched a campaign for worldwide narcotics traffic control that would extend through the years in an unbroken diplomatic sequence from the League of Nations to the present efforts of the United Nations.[6]

Dr. Hamilton Wright, father of narcotics control.

The appointment of Dr. Hamilton Wright as the opium commissioner in the U.S. State Department was probably more significant to the development of a domestic drug control policy than the convening of the Opium Commission in Shanghai. This ambitious bureaucrat seized his moment on the world stage with all the zeal of a reformer and the tenacity of a bull dog. Dr. Musto credits Wright for the eventual passage of the first federal drug control legislation. The anti-narcotics campaign in America had several motivations. Appeasement of China was certainly one factor for officials of the State Department. Hamilton Wright, the department's opium commissioner, thought the whole matter could be "used as oil to smooth the troubled water of our aggressive commercial policy there."[7] Wright was the prime mover for domestic drug control legislation, and believed that it was necessary if we were going to obtain international cooperation for an Opium Treaty. According to Dr. Musto: "After his return from Shanghai, Wright labored to craft a comprehensive federal anti narcotics law. In his path loomed the problem of States' rights. The health professionals were considered a major cause of patient addiction. Yet, how could federal law interfere with the prescribing practices of physicians or require that pharmacists keep records? Wright settled on the federal government's power to tax. After prolonged bargaining with pharmaceutical, import, export and medical interests, the result was the Harrison [Narcotics] Act of, December 17, 1914."[8]

The Enemy Is Us

Drugs—A moral evil, but not the major problem of the day.

It is important for the reader to understand that the motivating force for drug control in the United States <u>did not</u> arise because of a monumental problem with drug addictions within our society. This is not to say that there was no drug problem, but rather that society in early 20th century America discreetly handled its problem drug users. Many of those who were unable to break their dependency on drugs remained relatively productive, and maintained a respectable lifestyle while under the care of their physicians. Charitable doctors assisted those addicts without resources, or they were treated in public drug clinics that frequently administered drugs without charge. The few incorrigible "dopers" in a community became a task for the local police, and managing these addicts was frustrating. It was probably this frustration that caused exasperated public officials to resort to punitive measures when they began to enforce the drug ban.

The strategy to enforce the opium ban in the Philippines was never successful. Widespread opium smuggling in the archipelago kept the drug flowing to the users, but the agencies charged with enforcement of the ban persisted with the policy. To admit to their lack of success would have resulted in the loss of bureaucratic careers. A strategy to cut off supply consequently became the cornerstone of our present drug enforcement program and now, 90 years later, the United States government is still dependent upon the cooperation of foreigners to enforce the ban on drugs.

A front page story in the Miami Herald on, February 13, 1995, headlined, "Drug war ally may be dumped," illustrates this continuing problem: "Senior U.S. drug fighting officials are privately urging that President Clinton refuse to certify Bogota's anti-narcotics efforts as acceptable when he reports to Congress next month. ... 'The interagency anti-drug community has lost total confidence in Colombia,' said one U.S. official. ...[Colombia's] envoys gently deflect U.S. criticism back on America, saying supply follows demand." The United States followed through on its threat by decertifying Colombia in 1996 and declaring President Ernesto Samper persona non grata, dramatically demonstrating how the War on Drugs sours relations with otherwise friendly nations.

Ironically, drug prohibition was unnecessary to curb drug addiction in the United States, since the addiction rate was in a <u>steady decline</u> before any controls were in place. As this nation moved into the last decade of the 19th century, there was a growing concern by public health officials and city fathers across the nation over the proliferation of narcotics use and the rising number of drug habitués. There was strong criticism of the medical profession for over-prescribing habit-forming drugs and for the indifference of some physicians to the consequences of prolonged use of these substances. Patent medicines were experiencing booming growth, and the closely guarded contents of proprietaries remained secret. Concerned health officials warned the public that the contents of these medications were heavily weighted with alcohol, opium, and cocaine, and they cautioned against over reliance on these unproven remedies. The public responded to these warnings and the use of addicting drugs began to drop.

Professor Musto's examination of opium tariff records shows a steady increase in imports during the latter half of the 19th century, with the peak in per capita imports of opium occurring in 1896. After that time, the U.S.A. had a steady decline in opium imports until the Harrison Narcotics Act rendered these records valueless for further analysis. In 1902, an American Pharmaceutical Association Committee estimated about 200,000 opium addicts in a population of 79 million, or a 0.25% addiction rate. Even the pessimistic Dr. Hamilton Wright estimated only 175,000 opium addicts in a population of 90 million in 1909, or a 0.18% addiction rate. This is further evidence of a declining addict population after 1896.[9]

The Pure Food and Drug Act of 1906, requiring manufacturers to list the medicine contents on the package, was a positive and effective step in reducing use of narcotics and cocaine. Sales of patent medicines containing narcotics fell by one-third in the four years following enactment of the Pure Food and Drug Act, even as the sales of all proprietaries continued to rise dramatically. Articles in popular periodicals and medical journals educated and enlightened the public on the consequences of prolonged or heavy use of habit-forming drugs. Once informed, most people were able to stop the use of medications heavily laden with narcotics

The American society in the first two decades of this century was largely a vibrant, prosperous, and thriving society. Drug use by American citizens was a moral concern, but the drug problem of that day did not disrupt their economy, or domestic tranquillity, as America's drug problem does today. Congress in 1914 never intended a complete prohibition of drugs, but left their use chiefly in the hands of the physicians. The Harrison Act as originally written, limited the amount of narcotics used in proprietary medicines and banned cocaine in these medications altogether. It restricted the disbursement of both cocaine and narcotics to purchases by a physician's prescription. But the practical significance of the Act was to be debated for the next five years by the various groups affected.

The Harrison Act presented a curious dilemma for those addicted to drugs. Cocaine and heroin were still legal when prescribed in good faith by a physician, but could no longer be purchased over-the-counter. Conflicting interpretations of the Act erupted between the medical community and the Bureau of Internal Revenue, which was assigned to enforcement. Dr. Musto describes the conflict: "In a revealing letter to a woman who had taken morphine for many years and now complained that her supply would be cut off because of the Harrison Act, the Surgeon General replied in March 1915 that the act was intended simply to gather information and she could continue to receive her morphine from her physician. However, the Bureau of Internal Revenue, took a somewhat more stringent view. It prepared to bring action against druggists and physicians as well as addicts who were violating the bureau's understanding of the Harrison Act's moral principle—that taking narcotics for other than medicinal purposes was harmful and should be prevented."[10]

Agents of the Internal Revenue Service (IRS) believed that if they did not have police power under the Act to regulate the physician's prescription of narcotics, then unscrupulous physicians would be the benefactors of a highly profitable monopoly. Unscrupulous dope doctors did appear on the scene to write prescriptions to anyone for a fee. It is interesting that the simple requirement for a prescription to issue narcotics and cocaine resulted in America's first black market in drugs—albeit a black market in illicit prescriptions. The United States Supreme Court, by a seven to two vote, ruled against the IRS (U.S. v. Jin Fuey Moy) in a 1916 decision that upheld the doctor's prerogative to prescribe any drug he deemed necessary. The IRS finally obtained the ruling they wanted in 1919 in another case (Webb et al. v. U.S..). The Supreme Court essentially reversed its earlier decision and prohibited the prescribing of narcotics or cocaine solely to maintain a habitual user in his addiction.

Bugler, Sound Retreat

In his book *The American Disease*, the insightful Dr. Musto gives us a revealing description of the major players and the changing mood of America in that period between the Jin Fuey Moy decision in 1916, and the abrupt about face of the Supreme Court with its attack on addiction in 1919. He names these three major events that changed the mood of America: "World War I had been fought, the 18th Amendment had been adopted, and the liberalizing movements of LaFollette, Theodore Roosevelt, and Wilson had declined into fervent and intolerant nationalism. As a corollary perhaps to the last change came an enormous fear of Bolsheviks and anarchists, which has been termed the Red Scare of 1919-20. ...Having already been defined by most Americans as immoral or at least the cause of wasted lives, addiction by 1918 was perceived as a threat to the national war effort. Anything so perceived was likely to be in trouble."[11]

Prohibition—the beginning of repressive government in America.

A handful of dogged IRS bureaucrats set about to enforce their hard-nosed position by targeting doctors, and effectively eliminated all medical treatment for drug addiction. After 144 years of legitimacy, overnight the drug user was a criminal. What had been a medical problem for health professionals to prevent, control, and treat, was now in the domain of the law enforcers to punish with arrests, fines, incarceration, and confiscation of property. In the first decade of drug prohibition, half of the federal prison population was there for violation of the Harrison Narcotics Act. Some people interpret this information to mean that drugs cause crime. Yet, drug related crimes before prohibition were negligible. In reality, our drug policies have made criminals of a large section of our population whose offense is foolish and self-destructive behavior.

The enforcement of drug prohibition during the 1920s was overshadowed by the government's greater enforcement effort against the highly organized trafficking in illegal alcohol. Drugs remained a minor problem even after alcohol repeal and up to the 1960s. Chapter 1 gives some of the reasons for increased drug use in the stormy Sixties. On the supply side, huge profits and Mafia connections are cited. On the demand side, a decline in traditional values is blamed primarily.

The Enemy Is Us

In considering why both buying and selling of harmful drugs have increased since the 1960s, it is instructive to compare the past 35 years with the Great Depression and World War II. During the Depression of the 1930s, hard times did not bring high drug use, widespread dope peddling, or crime committed to obtain drugs. These harmful behaviors also did not increase significantly during World War II or even the Korean War. For the most part, responsibility and morality were cherished characteristics of the American people during those periods. Irresponsible behavior such as casual drug use—let alone the peddling of dope—is minimal in a society that adheres to traditional values. What changed?

Some observers, like the author of this book, place most of the blame on the changing views espoused by many of America's cultural leaders. These, at their worst, glorified a rejection of accepted norms of behavior and underlying religious tenets. Or, at their best, many cultural leaders simply advocated relative values. Self-gratification was celebrated by extreme cultural relativists. Other observers favor more social explanations. During World War II and into the Korean War—despite some dissatisfaction—the citizenry felt united in a struggle against tyranny. The Cold War failed to elicit this unity, while the Vietnam War inspired much open opposition. Meanwhile, scandals among high political and financial leaders bred cynicism. Despite a generally high level of prosperity, substantial pockets of poverty remained. Unlike the unemployed of the Great Depression—sometimes as numerous as 25 percent of the workforce—many of the postwar poor have lost hope. Hopelessness is cited by many authorities as a frequent reason for drug abuse in the slums. Drug selling—along with "turf wars"—is explained by cynicism. Your author recognizes the sincerity of readers who emphasize social conditions over the moral climate, yet those differences are fundamental. The United States cannot achieve a united course of action to attack drug abuse in this nation by either moral or social prescriptions alone. Stephen Covey's approach to problem-solving seems appropriate in this instance.[12] Seek first the interest of the other party; look for an arrangement that is best for us all; then we can move to synergy. What neither group can achieve alone, together we can succeed in attaining.

Bugler, Sound Retreat

Liberty and freedom flourish under free enterprise.

The Soviet Union chose a wrong direction when that nation moved toward communism after the revolution that overthrew the Czar. In the early years of the revolutionary experiment, Lenin admitted to his friend Armand Hammer, the American industrialist, that communism was not working. Lenin died shortly thereafter, so we will never know if he would have tried to change the government. It would be seventy years before the Soviet Union acknowledged its mistake by overthrowing the communists. That drama is still playing, but we can expect the new nation, or nations, to be something other than the old communist model—hopefully, a society more free. At the time the Russian revolutionaries chose communism, America's political leaders sought to eliminate the social problem of alcoholism and drug abuse by prohibiting the manufacture and sale of alcohol, narcotics, and cocaine[13]. As communism appeared to be the answer for the Russians, prohibition was thought to be the solution to our problem. This is not an attempt to compare prohibition to communism, but to point out that both nations made choices that were revolutionary and unproved. There was no precedent for either nation's actions. Now that we have the evidence from the past seventy-five years, clearly neither communism nor prohibition can be successful in a free `society.

Government interventions in the market place, whether it is through price controls, subsidies, or prohibition, distorts market forces and creates opportunities for criminals and the unethical. President Reagan repealed his predecessor's oil price controls, whereupon the great oil shortage with price gouging of the Seventies became the world oil glut with low prices of the Eighties. Commodity subsidies are designed to stabilize the commodities markets, but result in over-production, financial windfalls to wealthy producers, and budgetary shortfalls to the government—shortfalls that must be paid by the taxpayers. Government regulations and controls can cause unintended consequences. Controls, when required, should be carefully considered for side effects.

Congress conducted hearings in 1994 to consider regulating tobacco as a drug. Some people wanted to ban tobacco altogether. Joseph Califano, the former HEW Secretary, urged a Senate panel to place at least a $2 tax on each pack of cigarettes to discourage smoking. One hopes that neither the cigarette ban nor the excessive tobacco tax becomes law. Punitive actions such as these to correct behavior always cause a backlash, and over time are usually counter-productive. Americans should not lose sight of the fact that their anti-smoking program works well without prohibition, or prohibitive taxes. As shown later in this chapter, the anti-smoking campaign is succeeding. The proportion of American adults who smoke cigarettes dropped from 43% in 1965 to 25% in 1993, according to the U.S. Office on Smoking and Health.[14] Drug prohibition with its punitive enforcement measures was the mistake of an earlier America and needs correcting.

Sound taps, bugler—The Noble Experiment is dead.

Policy makers felt that criminal elements could be controlled by strong enforcement of the Volstead Act. To their consternation, illegal alcohol trafficking led to criminal gangs becoming organized on a national scale for the first time in our history. We learned that prohibition did not stop the drinking habits of a large segment of the American public. It also gave the underworld a lucrative business enterprise that made them a powerful and corrupting influence in our society. Drug prohibition has followed the same path.

A disturbing new element has appeared in the war on drugs that was not present during alcohol prohibition—youth gangs devoted to drug trafficking. ABC Evening News on February 8, 1995, documented the spreading activities of major large city gangs, such as the Los Angeles Crips and Bloods and the Chicago Gangster Disciples. These gangs are establishing sub-chapters of their drug-selling operations thousands of miles from their home bases by recruiting and financing local youths in moderate-size cities. Beside these large juvenile gangs, we see individual youths assisting drug dealers and frequently engaged in selling drugs to other juveniles. Kids, particularly the inner-city minorities, have become the labor force for the drug sub-culture.

The U.S. Congress legislated drug prohibition to reduce the use of narcotics and cocaine in the population. To the contrary, attempts to enforce prohibition increased the addiction rate by threefold, and created corollary problems of crime including killings, overcrowded prisons, and public corruption on a scale that never before existed. When they enacted drug prohibition, Congress forced legitimate businesses to retire from the socially unacceptable part of the drug market as discussed at the end of this chapter. The socially unacceptable use of drugs was driven underground into the hands of criminals. Finally, our government lost the ability to regulate or control drug use—except at the point of a gun barrel. This chapter is not an argument for condoning psychoactive drug use; rather it is a plea to Congress to retreat from a wrong direction, repeal drug prohibition and replace it with programs from our experience that have worked. Why are we hung up on drug prohibition? It took only thirteen years for our nation to acknowledge that alcohol prohibition was not working, and to repeal it.[15]

Sound retreat, bugler, we are attacking the wrong enemy.

It was painful to watch C-SPAN on February 10, 1995, when it televised the National Drug Control Strategy session before the Senate Judiciary Committee. This was not a strategy session, but a group of despondent officials rehashing old ideas and programs that their own figures demonstrate are not working. Not one new program was suggested. To everyone's dismay, not one new idea was advanced. The senators vowed to spend more money for extra policemen and more jails. As usual, the targeted enemy was the supplier of illicit drugs instead of the real enemy, the user who creates the demand.

America's young men are dying in foreign jungles fighting criminal drug lords whose only concern is for money, power, and all the influence that money can buy. At home, police officers and drug enforcement agents are being killed in their running battle with the drug cartel's army of drug dealers and drug gangs. Their crossfire kills innocent civilian bystanders daily. Here the author must speak editorially. America's greatest concern is not drugs or addicts. We can handle these. It's the guns and violence from drug traffickers in our neighborhoods that we most fear, and drug prohibition is the reason these dealers are on our streets.

A plane crash killed five U.S. Drug Enforcement Agency agents the last weekend of August 1994 on a desolate Peruvian mountain ridge. They were volunteers on a mission that meant constant danger. It was a reconnaissance flight as a part of "Operation Snowcap," a cocaine suppression program in Peru and Bolivia. Earlier that month, America lost a paratrooper who was working with the Chilean drug forces. "They took the risks," their colleagues said, "because the drug war is crucial to their country." Attorney General Reno praised them for doing the vital work of the nation. Dare any government official call this drug war crucial or vital when it only worsens the drug problem?

The Enemy Is Us

America's drug war should not be fought in the jungles of Colombia, Peru, and Bolivia, or in American streets and neighborhoods. This drug war has never obtained a positive result and is an endless conflict with no value. At home, it is the catalyst for crime that brings fear to communities, saps economic vitality, and depletes the national treasury. It is time to repeal prohibition, declare peace, and bind up the nation's wounds. Drug peace will bring America a <u>lower addiction rate</u>, <u>less crime</u>, <u>less corruption</u>, <u>less bureaucracy</u>, <u>reduced government spending,</u> and <u>more revenue from drug taxes</u>.

Congress is in the Denial Stage.

Congress denies that prohibition is the cause of the nation's drug problem, as an alcoholic denies that liquor is the cause of his problems. Like the alcoholic, Congress must get beyond the denial stage before it can take the first step toward a solution. Members of Congress so fear that their constituents will label them as "Soft" on drugs that it has become difficult to have a calm and reasoned discussion about the Federal Drug Control Policy.

Alcohol, a mood altering drug, costs our nation 25,000 deaths annually and an estimated $100 billion.[16] It is one of America's major medical problems, greater by far than the medical problem from drug abuse. Yet the United States made the decision to repeal alcohol prohibition and to try to discourage abusive drinking, while leaving alcoholic beverages legally available, because prohibition created greater problems.

Nicotine is the most deadly addictive, psychoactive drug in the nation and remains legal to this day. Second hand cigarette smoke causes over 50,000 deaths each year in the United States, not to mention the more than 400,000 death annually attributed to cigarette smoking. The annual cost of diseases relating to smoking is estimated at $50 billion. Former Surgeon General Koop called nicotine our most addictive drug, yet cigarettes are not even classified as a drug. All levels of government in the U.S. now regulate where and when one smokes. Cigarette advertising on TV was banned in 1965. A Public Health counter-advertising program was initiated and cigarette smoking began to decrease. As noted earlier, cigarette smoking among the adult population dropped from 43% in 1965 to 25% in 1993. The percentage of everyday smokers fell even more, to 20.4%. The statistics are from the Office on Smoking and Health, in the Department of Health and Human Services—not the Internal Revenue Service or the Justice Department. One suggestion advanced to further reduce smoking in America is to prevent tobacco corporations from using any form of advertising or promotion. The United States is effectively dealing with the smoking problem as a public health problem without prohibiting the individual from smoking or tobacco companies from selling their product.

Analyze the problem objectively—without hysteria.

The present drug policy has driven drug users underground into a subculture where it is difficult to change social attitudes. Politicians have been reluctant to condemn their drug using constituents, but rather blame the foreign drug cartels and the drug dealers for addicting our citizens. As one observer writes: "For almost a century American anti drug policy has blamed foreigners for the American drug disease, thus preserving the myth that Americans are naturally good but corrupted by evil foreigners."[17] The solution to America's drug problem is in the U.S.A.

Drs. Gabriel G. Nahas[18] and Mark S. Gold[19] are two dedicated proponents of our present drug policies. In separate books, both express their concern and fear over the growing use of cocaine in our society. Their concern is respected, as well as their expertise in pharmacology and drug addiction, but the evidence shows that their faith in drug prohibition has been misplaced. We could probably tolerate some crime and corruption that goes with prohibition, if it significantly reduced drug use, but it does not.

In his book *Cocaine: The Great White Plague* Dr. Nahas, calculates that in 1910 there were 250,000 habitual users of opiates and cocaine in the nation.[20] He arrives at this 250,000 figure by adding his estimate of 75,000 habitual cocaine users to Dr. Hamilton Wright's 1910 estimate of 175,000 habitual users of the opiates in a population of about 90 million.[21] This appears to be a fair calculation. In 1990, however, the Office of National Drug Control Policy reported approximately 1.8 million hard-core cocaine addicts and an additional 600,000 heroin addicts in the United States population of approximately 250 million.[22] This equates to an addiction rate of 0.96% in 1990, or more than three times the addiction rate of 0.28% in 1910. Evidently, unrestricted availability of drugs in the legal drug market before 1915 was not a factor in the rate of drug use, but the social consensus against the use of addictive drugs was primary.

Billions are spent at home trying to sweep drug dealers from our streets and neighborhoods. Over a third of the municipal police efforts and over half of the incarcerations are drug related. Each year of the War on Drugs saw an increase in violence, guns, killings and imprisonments. But the worst aspect of this drug war is that it has enabled inner-city juvenile gangs to flourish. ABC News reports that each of these major gangs brings in profits of $500 million, and some are controlled by hardened convicts from their prison cells.[23] The reporter interviewed one of the teenage sellers who claims to make $500 per day. If he sells only 200 days a year he will make $100,000--tax free. You can see why it is difficult for any kid to say NO to drugs, when prohibition provides such an irresistible opportunity!

The Clinton Plan

This is the Clinton plan according to Drug Czar Lee P. Brown, in a letter to the Miami Herald on August 3, 1994: "The 1994 National Drug Control Strategy makes treatment of chronic, hard-core drug users one of its top priorities. This administration also realizes the importance of a balanced approach to the drug crisis. Treatment alone cannot solve the drug problem. Supply control also plays an important role. We will continue to have effective supply reduction programs, such as interdiction and source country programs." General McCaffrey succeeded Brown as Drug Czar in 1996, but has not made any significant changes in policy. He has only promised to spend more money and try harder.

We can take some comfort in that President Clinton's approach will give greater priority to treatment of chronic, hard-core drug users, but one has to be disappointed that the changes are minimal with no new approaches to drug control. His administration will still rely heavily on law enforcement and supply side suppression tactics as shown in his 1994 $30-billion crime bill that calls for 100,000 more police officers on the streets and many more federal prisons. Sadly, the new Republican-controlled 104th Congress is decidedly moving in the wrong direction, calling for more law enforcement and prisons, while cutting funds for education and treatment. Law enforcement has not worked to reduce drug addiction and should not be a part of a new drug control strategy.

Finding a new strategy.

Some have suggested that the United States should execute all drug traffickers and addicts to ensure a drug free society as they do in totalitarian countries, such as China, Iran, and Saudi Arabia. On, January 30, 1995, Saudi Arabia beheaded four drug smugglers, bringing to 13 the number of people punished by the Islamic form of execution in four days.[24] Executions for drug use and trafficking in these totalitarian countries are a common occurrence. Even beheading does not eliminate all drug smuggling. To institute this form of drug control obviously would mean yielding precious freedom and individual rights guaranteed by the U.S. Constitution to a totalitarian police state. Few murderers are executed in the U.S.A.; yet some people would execute a person for snorting cocaine or injecting heroin. Are Americans going to kill the few foolish citizens who fail to exercise civic responsibility or personal control? Or will they seek a more humane and less violent way as they do for alcoholics—using education, persuasion, training, coercion, voluntary confinement to a treatment center, and, as a last resort, incarceration?

If members of Congress would research alternatives to prohibition and hard-nosed law enforcement, they would conclude that whatever policy they choose, it will work better in a legal drug environment. The following chapters will discuss arguments for legalizing psychoactive drugs—also prospects, problems, and proponents of legalization. Here prevention and treatment of drug abuse are discussed.

Many citizens, who would hasten to assist an alcoholic in overcoming his addiction, will hesitate or back away from assisting a drug addict in a similar circumstance. The alcoholic is in every way just as addicted, inflicts just as much hurt on those around him, and is just as pitiful a human being as any drug addict. But being an alcoholic is not a criminal act, and he doesn't have to consort with the underworld to continue his destructive habit. Also it is more comfortable for others to work with the alcoholic within the confines of normal society. The drug addict can place his benefactor in a more uncomfortable environment than an alcoholic who has "fallen off the wagon." The recovering drug addict who goes seeking drugs subjects himself to arrest for a drug crime, or may become the victim of a crime. The benefactor might have to go among the criminal element in unsavory sections of the city while attempting to keep his beneficiary from falling back in with the drug subculture. The drug addict can only obtain his drugs from criminals, and this fact alone binds him to the drug underworld.

Here the author must editorialize again. Despite the inconveniences and risks, every one of us has a moral obligation to help a neighbor who has strayed into substance abuse or fallen on drug addiction. Our institutions—churches, schools, hospitals, and courts—have a duty in our society to help and encourage sobriety and clean living for those who have been overtaken by substance abuse. As important as it is to have compassion, it is more important that your compassion is not misdirected. Marvin Olasky, in his book *The Tragedy of American Compassion*, traces the history of charitable assistance in this nation for the last 300 years. He decries the change in care-giving from an earlier time, when attention was given to the personality and spirituality of the whole person, usually in a one-on-one relationship. He compares that with the impersonal attention and concern only for the beneficiary's material needs in the large federal assistance programs.[25] Perhaps the government can provide a better approach to community care-giving to drug abusers in its new drug policy—a policy with less direction from Washington-based bureaucrats.

Unfortunately charitable giving per household declined 24 percent from 1989 to 1993, while donated volunteer time dropped 5 percent, according to a respected survey. At the same time, new church programs were started. For instance, Rev. George Clements, a Chicago priest, launched "One Church, One addict," a program now in three states. Significantly, Catholic Charities USA, "the nation's largest private social service network" received 65 percent of its 1993 budget from government grants and contracts—federal, state, and local.[26] For better or worse, modern Americans seem to want to combine private and public social programs, and this is not a new trend in America. Olasky found numerous instances going back to the 18th century where town councils authorized reimbursement to local citizens or organizations for expenses incurred in caring for orphans, needy persons, or families. It seems to matter little from whence the funds come, but it matters mightily as to how that care is provided. More on this in later chapters.

Drug addiction is only slightly related to the availability of any drug. The supply increases when there is a demand for these drugs in either a legal or an illegal market. America has seen drug addiction rates fall and rise in both legal and illegal drug markets. There was an unlimited supply of drugs in the legal markets before drug prohibition, and there is certainly a plethora of addicting drugs on our streets today. How then can one explain the fact that over 99% of the American population do not have a drug addiction problem in this illegal drug market—and even a greater ratio avoided addiction in the legal markets? <u>It is simply that the vast majority of Americans make a personal decision not to use these drugs</u>. Societal attitudes and personal responsibility, not availability, determine the amount of drug use in our nation. Americans are wasting a lot of time, money, and effort trying to suppress the drug supply.

The only wise move now is to acknowledge that prohibition was a mistake and to retreat from this failed experiment. Congress should close down the unproductive overseas drug war that saps the nation's strength, drains American treasure, and antagonizes nations that would like to be friendly. The first step is to eliminate the threat from the overseas drug cartel's minions. As the next chapter makes clear, it can be done with Congress's secret weapon without losing a man or costing a nickel.

4

NUKE THE DRUG CARTELS
Eliminating the drug cartels with our ultimate weapon

"Money, Money, Money, Money—It makes the world go around," sang Joel Grey and Liza Minnelli in the musical "Cabaret." Money also makes the drug world go around. It is the fuel that propels this international consortium of illegal drug producers, smugglers, dealers, and pushers. The drug lords will corrupt, maim, or murder, without hesitation, anyone who stands in the way of their enterprise. But without the continuous flow of huge profits, this illicit operation would have no prospect and would collapse of its own accord.

The drug cartels and their American henchmen, the drug dealers, are the greatest beneficiaries of our national drug strategy. When leaders of the Theodore Roosevelt Administration decided to prohibit opium in the Philippines in 1905, they could not have imagined that they were spawning a criminal malignancy that would eventually spread over the whole world, nor could they have envisioned the eventual social chaos that would occur as a result of their decision. Prohibition seemed such a simple, straightforward method to solve a sordid little social problem. However, it was evident shortly thereafter that enforcing the prohibition of opium smoking in the Philippines was more of a challenge than they had anticipated, and prohibition continued to be an enforcement problem long after those decision-makers' time on this earth.

Once the drug control plan was initiated, the next step was to make it work. Unfortunately, it has yet to work. As the reader will recall from the previous chapter, the planners hit upon the idea of controlling the supply of drugs by destroying drug crops and attacking trafficking in source nations. It is difficult for any strategic planner to imagine a more convoluted scheme then this process involving all the nations of the world to control drugs in the U.S.A. The process also requires the cooperating drug-producing countries to forgo a very lucrative business. Drug addiction was never a justification to send the United States armed forces and drug agents against foreign drug producers to control the supply of drugs to this nation. The United States did not have a drug problem of sufficient magnitude that required our State Department to initiate this complicated plan of international drug control.

The President's Commission on Organized Crime in 1986 stated that more than half of all organized crime revenues were believed to derive from the illicit drug business and could run as high as $50-billion annually.[1] By contrast, annual revenues from cigarette bootlegging, which persists principally because of differences among states in their cigarette tax rates, were estimated by this same Commission at between $200 million and $400 million. When bootlegging a legal drug, nicotine (tobacco), organized crime can only realize 1/1000th of the revenues it derives from illegal drugs. This statistic is even more remarkable when one considers that the number of nicotine addicts is twenty times greater than the number of narcotics and cocaine addicts combined. Ethan Nadelmann, formerly an Assistant Professor of Politics and Public Affairs at Princeton University and now Director of The Lindesmith Center, notes that the billions of dollars the United States spends on enforcing the drug laws amount to a subsidy of organized crime.[2]

A good strategy in any war is to press the attack at your enemy's most vulnerable point and destroy it. One need not be General Norman Schwarzkopf to appreciate the strategic importance of money as the fuel that runs the international drug cartels. As surely as the allies immobilized Rommel's panzer divisions in World War II by destroying his petroleum supply lines, the drug cartels' enterprise can be neutralized by eliminating the obscene profits from illegal drugs. Without firing a shot, without losing one man, without spending one dollar, and never having to leave the safety of the National Capitol, the U.S. Congress could employ a strategy using our ultimate drug war weapon to blast the overseas drug lords' smuggling operation right out of existence. Our ultimate weapon is repeal of prohibition!

In the Vietnam War, the American army was never sure which Vietnamese in the black pajamas belonged to the Viet Cong. The United States unwisely chose to fight a guerrilla war on the streets, in the villages, and in the jungles of South Vietnam one-on-one, and could never be sure as to who was the enemy until our side was fired upon. We are facing such an enemy in the War on Drugs, where the United States faces an international alliance of criminal armies operating covertly in most nations of the world. The drug traffickers and dealers blend in with the various populations and must be ferreted out one at a time. The cartels are well-financed and well-armed, and the American drug-using public is providing most of their money and resources. Ironically, Americans are financing both sides in the War on Drugs.

The Supply-Side Campaign.

Rensselaer W. Lee III, in *The White Labyrinth—Cocaine & Political Power*, has written a scholarly study that details the structure and power of the South American drug cartels. Asian drug lords are examined in *The Politics of Heroin* by Alfred W. McCoy, a professor at the University of Wisconsin. The present book will not dwell on the machinations of the illegal drug trade outside our borders, except to point out the folly of present U.S. policy that coerces foreign governments to serve in our War on Drugs. In his preface, Lee states that "Supply-side approaches, however, have obviously failed to stem the flow of cocaine into U.S. markets." [3] In his concluding chapter, McCoy writes: "As long as the demand for drugs in the cities of the First World continues to grow, Third World producers will find a way to supply their markets."[4] Lee's three conclusions about U.S. attempts to cut off cocaine in the Andes also applies to efforts to suppress heroin from Burma or hashish from the Middle East. He writes:

> First, the cocaine trade has altered irrevocably the economic and political landscape of the Andean countries. Cocaine traffickers constitute an interest group with extensive resources and political connections, just like the coffee barons of Colombia or the mining elites in Peru and Bolivia. Indeed, studies of these countries' development patterns, decision making processes, and relations with other countries are no longer possible without reference to coca and cocaine.

> Second, the drug war in South American source countries presents difficult if not unmanageable problems for both South American governments and the U.S. government. The drug war requires that Andean countries address a host of obstacles, such as national economic dependence on drugs, powerful narcotics lobbies, indifferent or hostile publics, weak political structures, and porous systems of criminal justice. In addition, other compelling U.S. interests in the region-such as promoting economic stability, preserving democracy or preventing the emergence of Marxist regimes

are not necessarily compatible with aggressive drug control programs.

Third, even with significant U.S. help, Andean governments will make little progress in controlling cocaine production. Eradication campaigns, occasional large drug busts, and a few major arrests (like the highly publicized arrests of Carlos Lehder in Colombia and Roberto Suarez in Bolivia) will continue in the Andean countries. Nonetheless, the basic structure of the cocaine industry—its agricultural base, manufacturing infrastructure, leadership, smuggling networks, and so on—will remain more or less intact. The corollary: Victory in the war against cocaine cannot be won in the jungles, shanty towns, and trafficking capitals of South American countries: only when Americans decide that they will no longer be the drug lords' customers will the industry collapse.[5]

Fighting the U.S. drug war overseas is far more extensive than most Americans realize. Every day there are dispatches from countries around the globe relating to the struggle to defeat the drug smugglers. All readers can recall the invasion of Panama, to break up the Medellin Cartel's drug conduit through that nation, and the spiriting away of Panama's president to stand trial in Miami for his drug crimes against the United States. Then there was the highly publicized campaign, inspired and financed by the United States, to bring the Medellin Cartel chief, Pablo Escobar, to justice. But even before Escobar's death in 1992, control of the Colombian cocaine trade had already shifted to the Cali Cartel. These vigorous efforts have been on going since the Nixon administration, and every day U.S. currency flows out of its treasury to fight the drug war. American personnel operating in these countries are facing death daily at the hands of the illegal drug operators. Yet, the nation has no beneficial results to show for such a major war that has lasted for more years than the combined total for all the other wars the United States has fought in this century.

An example of the United States' failed drug strategy in the Andean countries occurred in early 1994 when a leader of the Cali Cartel surrendered. Instead of congratulating or thanking Colombian authorities, U.S. drug agents expressed suspicion that surrendering traffickers would get short sentences and keep wealth and power after release from prison.[6]

The Enemy Is Us

A few days later, the U.S. law enforcement agencies suspended an evidence-sharing program with Colombia's Attorney General de Greiff, because of his alleged willingness to make accommodations with drug traffickers.[7] According to a news report: "De Greiff enraged some Colombian and U.S. officials by meeting secretly with Cali traffickers, who were seeking to negotiate lenient sentences in return for surrender. Worse, he has gone public with his doubts about whether the battle against trafficking is even winnable, suggesting that illicit narcotics should be legalized."[8]

Ramon Mestre, of the Miami Herald editorial board, interviewed Gustavo de Greiff in Mexico City in early 1995, where he was Colombia's ambassador to Mexico. Mestre wrote:

> ...once he was named attorney general, he discovered the contradictions inherent in an unwinnable drug war that helps weaken and corrupt Colombian society as it strengthens drug traffickers and the drug-control establishment.

> After his Baltimore talk on legalization, U.S. Attorney General Janet Reno read him the riot act, de Greiff says. He adds that she refused to consider his argument's possible merits and took the attitude that the War on Drugs rests on "reason of state."

> Reason of state often conceal the unreason of power....

Editor Mestre also wrote that de Greiff agreed with his observation "that there are three groups fiercely opposed to the legalization of drugs: First the drug dealers, who stand to lose their huge profits and influence; next, law-enforcement institutions whose very existence depends on the suppression of illegal narcotics; and finally, all those politicians, bankers, lawyers, business people, judges, cops, and journalists who are on the drug Mafia's' payroll."[9]

The illegal heroin network is graphically described by Professor McCoy: "Almost all of the world's illicit opium is grown in the narrow 4,500-mile stretch of mountains that extends across southern Asia from Turkey through Pakistan to Laos. Peasants and tribesmen of eight different nations harvest some 4,000 tons a year of raw opium ....A small percentage of these 4,000 tons is diverted from legitimate pharmaceutical production in Turkey, Iran, and India, but most of it is grown expressly for the international narcotics traffic...." Although the U.S. Central Intelligence Agency has denied McCoy allegations that CIA agents have used the illegal drug network for purposes of espionage and counter-insurgency, the accuracy of his description of the network has not been questioned.[10]

**"Where we are going we have no notion,
but isn't it wonderful to be in motion."**

During the author's military service, this little ditty was often recited whenever the outcome of our mission was uncertain and the leadership was obviously confused. It prompts another editorial comment. Our political leaders are giving us motion, and they have no notion as to where this War on Drugs will take us. We must ask the question, "Why are we putting American lives on the line in countries that do not want to cooperate with us in fighting America's drug war?" These countries have a thriving and lucrative business in supplying the Yankees with drugs. This aspect of the drug war makes the least sense, has been the least productive, and is the most expensive in lives, money, and effort. Even if other nations wanted to cooperate, the growing areas for coca and opium are often in the hands of outlaws, beyond the control of the legitimate governments of these nations.

A typical day in the U.S. drug war overseas is illustrated by these three news items on a single day, in 1991:

PANAMA-A disbanded military unit that defended former leader Gen. Manuel Antonio Noriega during two coup attempts is organizing to topple President Guillermo Endara....

PERU-The Bush administration plans to dispatch more than 50 military trainers to Peru to help the military to fight drug traffickers and guerrillas involved in producing and smuggling cocaine. .... Administration officials said the move reflected an emerging view that Lima was losing control of its Andean mountain provinces to drug barons and to Maoist Shining Path rebels, who protect the traffickers.

PARAGUAY-A Bolivian Air Force plane carrying 35 pounds of cocaine made an emergency landing in western Paraguay, and authorities Monday arrested the three people, including a lieutenant, aboard.[11]

Thus in one day, drug corruption in four Latin American countries was reported. Three other countries were added on a single day in 1995. A Honduran was the key link, U.S. officials reported, in setting up ties between Mexican traffickers and the Colombian cocaine cartels. The Colombians fly large shipments of cocaine to northern Mexico, where it is sneaked across the 2,000-mile border with the U.S.A. Mexican political stability is threatened by the drug lords. When top political leaders, including a candidate for Mexico's presidency, were assassinated in 1994, drug lords were widely blamed.[12] According to news reports, the Colombian cartels have made underworld contacts in Canada, in case the U.S.-Mexican border becomes smuggle-proof.

Pick up your morning paper today and you will probably find reference to similar incidents. The recent spectacle of Peruvian jet fighters firing upon an unarmed United States Air Force C-130 transport on a DEA mission in Peruvian airspace, killing one crew member and wounding three others, is difficult to comprehend. Thirty years of military flying experience makes it impossible for the author to accept this incident as a case of mistaken identity. It was too flagrant. This attack appears to be another example of Peruvian military leaders cooperating with the drug lords. There are dozens of such incidents that clearly show how the U.S. gets only lip service from government officials in the Andean countries. When reporters find foreign diplomats that will speak candidly, off the record, they say that the drug problem is the U.S.'s problem, and that their "cooperation" is an accommodation to keep the American dollars flowing. While taking American dollars on one hand, they are cooperating with the drug cartels on the other.

Wherever the U.S. State Department believes that it has leverage, there are attempts to pressure or cajole the foreign heads of state to eliminate drug production and trafficking in their nation, usually with the same results. For instance, when President Bush's Secretary of State, James Baker, visited Syria, Syrian officials made several arrests and burned 40 tons of hashish. But a top official told a Reuters Correspondent that this action was merely cosmetic. In Pakistan, a reformist prime minister, Benazir Bhutto, launched a campaign against heroin traffickers in 1989, with U.S. encouragement. But since the heroin trade now contributed one quarter of Pakistan's domestic product, she got nowhere.[13] In 1990, President Bush signed an anti-drug accord with the presidents of Bolivia, Colombia, and Peru. A year later, a Congressional aide called the results "fairly discouraging."[14]

A report by the Clinton Administration, appearing March 2, 1995, is even more revealing as to the status of the War on Drugs, and clearly it is not going the way our drug warriors had planned it:

> In its annual report to Congress on the performance of drug-producing and transit nations, the administration withheld full

certification of Colombia's anti-narcotic efforts for the first time since the evaluation process began in 1987. "We clearly do not feel at this point that the Colombian government is fully cooperating with us," said Robert Gelbard, the assistant secretary of state for international narcotics matters.

But at the same time the administration invoked the U.S. national interest as grounds for granting Colombia a waiver....Also issued national security waivers despite less-than-acceptable performances in the war against drugs were Bolivia and Peru, which account for 80 percent of the raw material for cocaine, and Paraguay, a growing transit point for cocaine and marijuana.

Of the 29 countries on the list, five countries were designated fully uncooperative in the war on narcotics: Syria, Iran, Burma, Nigeria and Afghanistan. Afghanistan, where a civil war makes any drug enforcement impossible, was the only newcomer to the list. But Gelbard said that Colombia, as the source of virtually all of the refined cocaine reaching U.S. cities, remains "the most critical country in terms of the United States government and the president's Western Hemisphere drug strategy.[15]

Supply-side suppression has failed.

The U.S.A. is no closer to eliminating the supplies of cocaine, heroin, or hashish then it was 10 years ago, or 20 years ago, or 75 years ago. But to the drug warriors, victory in the drug war is just around the corner. If the national leaders would be honest with themselves and the American people, they would admit that they cannot expect to be successful in suppressing foreign drug supplies even after another decade—if ever. The United States cannot expect that these countries will willingly fight its drug war and give up the enormous cash largess that flows to their countrymen from this lucrative operation, especially since a good bit of those profits goes into the pockets of government officials.

President Clinton has tried to convey a change in strategy in his first year in office to more emphasis on demand reduction at home by ordering a retrenchment in efforts to interdict drugs on the high seas and along overland drug-smuggling routes. Yet his reduction amounted to only $100 million, or about 7% of the previous year's budget for this effort. By even the most optimistic estimates, our interdiction operations intercept only 10% of the drugs being shipped. The repeal of drug prohibition would allow the U.S. to scrap all of a very expensive and ineffective interdiction operation by the U.S. Coast Guard, Navy, Marine Corps, Air Force, and Customs Service.

The strategy to suppress drugs at their source, and the attempt to cut the drug supply line, has not seriously affected the supply of drugs on streets. Ted Koppel, on Nightline, ABC TV, April 6, 1995, quoted government figures on cocaine prices in the U.S. Since 1982 cocaine prices have fallen from a range of $45-$55 thousand per kilo to a range of $10-$40 thousand per kilo. Falling prices indicate that the drug is in plentiful supply. In spite of the greater supply, easy availability, and lower price, cocaine use fell from 1982 to 1990--more evidence that those three factors do not necessarily equate to higher drug use. There is no effective way to eliminate the illegal supply of drugs as long as prohibition laws encourage smuggling and yield such lucrative returns to the smugglers. The drug war also gives leverage to source and transit countries to extract money from this nation as a condition for their cooperation.

A strategy that went awry

Thomas W. Lippman reviewed a book for the Washington Post written by Robert S. McNamara, who played a central role in the Vietnam War as the Defense Secretary in the John F. Kennedy's and Lyndon Johnson's administrations:[16]

> As recounted by McNamara in *In Retrospect: The Tragedy and Lessons of Vietnam*, the war could and should have been avoided and should have been halted at several key junctures after it started.

> According to McNamara, he and other senior advisers to President Lyndon B. Johnson failed to head it off through ignorance, inattention, flawed thinking, political expediency and lack of courage.

> Even when he and Johnson's other aides knew that their Vietnam strategy had little chance of success, McNamara writes, they pressed ahead with it, ravaging the land and sending young Americans to their deaths year after year, because they had no other plan.

Nuke the Drug Cartels

Were the reader to substitute "War on Drugs" where the word "Vietnam" appears in the above paragraphs he or she would have an exact parallel to what has happened, and what is happening, to the United States today.   Instead of the notorious body-counts of the Vietnam War, tons of dope destroyed are now trumpeted. But the killing fields remain.   Professor Milton Friedman calculates that 10,000 Americans are killed annually in the War on Drugs. While McNamara played a central role in the Vietnam War, he had four presidents and some of the "best and brightest" in the Kennedy administration to share the blame and the shame with him. In the overall scheme of things, this author's combat role in the Vietnam War was minor, but it was a motivation to study and try to understand the political considerations involved. Before the Vietnam War the military services had issued studies on the strategic lessons of the Korean War. The number one lesson? The United States should never engage in a land war of attrition in Asia. Is there not a similar lesson about prohibition.

ABC News ran a special program hosted by Catherine Crier, on April 6, 1995, entitled, "America's War on Drugs—Searching for a Solution." It was a reasonably balanced presentation that explored much of the current thinking on this subject from the defenders of the status quo to the Libertarian proponents of a laissez-faire drug market.   It was disconcerting to hear William Bennett, the former drug czar, defend the status quo by stiffening his neck and declaring, "You will never persuade the citizens of this country, never, that they should legalize drugs."(His emphasis, not mine.) Mr. Bennett would do well to recall the words of Senator Morris Shepard of Texas, who had co-authored the alcohol Prohibition Amendment. Only two years before the vote to repeal Prohibition, he confidently asserted: "There is as much chance of repealing the Eighteenth Amendment as there is for a humming-bird to fly to the planet Mars with the Washington Monument tied to its tail."[17]

We don't have to reinvent the wheel.

The United States does not have to perform an expensive, drawn-out research program to find a logical, efficient, and cost-effective system for drug control. An honest evaluation of America's experience during the past 100 years in attempting to regulate and control addictive drugs (narcotics, cocaine, alcohol, and nicotine) is the only research laboratory required.   Early in this century national leaders rejected the free enterprise system—under which drug addiction rates were steadily falling—to experiment with the utopian dream of an *alcohol-and-drug-free America.* That dream turned into a nightmare when organized crime gained control of the alcohol and narcotics trade.

Congress, in collaboration with the state governors, should concentrate on "How" to frame its drug policy. Should Congress again establish a National Advisory Council to study the problem, as it did in 1972, its first advice to the new council should be to study the lessons learned from the 1972 effort. The reader can see a wider discussion of the council's activities in Chapter 7. The chairman of the council, Professor James Q. Wilson, took pride in the fact that the council ignored Professor Milton Friedman's criticisms of President Nixon's War on Drugs in a Newsweek column, and rejected Friedman's plea to legalize drugs. Following are Professor Friedman's more recent comments on that incident, and the government's drug policy architects would do well to consider his advice:

I reread the column that I published in Newsweek criticizing [President Nixon's] actions. Very few words in that column would have to be changed for it to be publishable today. The problem then was primarily heroin and the chief source of the heroin was Marseilles. Today, the problem is cocaine from Latin America. Aside from that, nothing would have to be changed.

Here it is [more than] twenty years later. What were then predictions are now observable results. As I predicted in that column, on the basis primarily of our experience with Prohibition, drug prohibition has not reduced the number of addicts appreciably if at all and has promoted crime and corruption.

Why is it that the only observable effect on policy of the conversion of predictions into results has been that the government digs itself deeper and deeper into a bigger and bigger hole and spends more and more of your and my money doing harm? Why is it? That's both the most discouraging feature of our experience and also the most intriguing intellectual puzzle.

I want to examine the puzzle that I raised. And in doing so, I'm going to rely on an adage that Bartlett traces back to 325 B.C.: "Cobbler, stick to your last." My last is economics, the

58

study of how society organizes its limited resources to meet the many and varied wants of its members. Fundamentally, society's resources can be organized in only one of two ways, or by some mixture of them.

One way is by market mechanisms from the bottom up. The other way is by command from top down. The market is one mechanism. Authoritarian organization—the military is a clear example—is the other.... The fundamental problem we face is not the war on drugs....The war on drugs and the harm which it does are simply manifestations of a much broader problem: the substitution of political mechanisms for market mechanisms in a wide variety of areas....The war on drugs is a failure because it is a socialist enterprise.[18]

Private enterprise is the American way.

The United States can literally go "back to the future," to a time before federal drug controls and the passage of the Harrison Narcotics Act on December 17, 1914. That should be the starting point to craft a wiser policy based on accumulated experience in controlling addictive substances. Congress should start by revoking all laws pertaining to drug prohibition, and after carefully installing only those controls that have worked in the past to reduce drug use, return recreational drugs to legitimate private enterprise. The predictions on the War on Drugs made in 1972 by Nobel laureate Milton Friedman, have proven out

Unless drug production, trade, and consumption are returned to a legitimate status there is no way to avoid a protracted and costly war with the international criminal drug syndicates. As long as any part of drug commerce is illegal—production, trade, or consumption—criminal activity will occur to sustain the illegal portion of the drug enterprise. Prohibition made no sense for alcohol, and it makes no sense for drugs. As reported in Chapter 3, drug addictions on a per-capita basis have increased under prohibition, so why is there a hesitancy about the repeal of prohibition?

Some say that repeal is too revolutionary, that we should reform by degrees. Harm reduction is the buzzword heard most often among the drug-policy reformers these days. Many would do things in an evolutionary fashion, such as authorizing marijuana for medical use, or establishing needle exchange programs to reduce the exposure to AIDS.

59

Some suggest decriminalizing only soft drugs and marijuana. Others want to go as far as decriminalizing <u>possession</u> of small amounts of hard drugs, yet keeping <u>production</u> and <u>trade</u> illegal—as Colombia did in 1994. Many point to the Netherlands as a model, where leniency is the policy. There all aspects of the drug trade remain illegal, but the police look the other way as long as users are discreet and dealers keep their activities low-key. However, the evolutionary approach does not address the prime culprit in America's drug agony—crime. It leaves intact the cartels, dealers, and drug gangs—with the accompanying killings, violence, corruption, and the attempted pushing of drugs onto everyone, including children at school.

This nation repealed alcohol prohibition in a single step that some considered a bold move and that worried many. But repeal was not as daring as one might imagine since it came less than 14 years after the beginning of prohibition. Most of the population in 1932 had clear memories of legal alcohol, so the American people voted confidently for a return to legal alcohol. None of the nation's leaders today have any memory of legal narcotics and cocaine, but they do have the history and records from pre-prohibition days that clearly show that drug addiction, while a moral concern, caused no significant crime problem nor created the major social disruptions experienced today.

A full-scale discussion of possible drug-control scenarios would be premature at this point, but it is the right time to establish basic guidelines for a new drug control policy for the United States. As stated previously, to keep organized crime out of the drug market, adult Americans must have legal access to, and factual information on, all drugs without undue restriction. In a free nation the individual is responsible for his or her choices and behavior. The government should not intervene unless the individual's actions injure someone else or place that person in harm's way.

The Ultimate Weapon—Repeal.

The Ultimate Weapon (repeal of prohibition), would again authorize legitimate U.S. pharmaceutical manufacturers to produce and supply heroin, cocaine, and marijuana to legitimate retail outlets in the United States. This trade had always been conducted as a normal, legitimate business in the private sector for the 144-year history of the United States before drug prohibition. By abolishing the prohibition against narcotics, cocaine, and marijuana, the United States can dislodge the foreign criminal drug cartels and replace them with legitimate U.S. manufacturers that import these drugs from legitimate foreign producers. The criminal drug cartels will then strangle like a person who has had the platform sprung from under him and is left dangling from a scaffold at the end of a rope. With the criminal drug empire destroyed at its roots, the cartel's dealers and pushers in the U.S. would wither and die.

The questions about life in the United States after the repeal of drug prohibition are discussed at length in Chapter 7, where historical evidence is presented that points to a lower rate of drug addictions in a legitimate drug market. The reader is asked to accept, for the purposes of discussion, that the rate of drug addictions will decrease; or in the worst case, will not rise significantly above today's rate. With this premise accepted for the moment, consider, the logic of repealing drug prohibition.

1. Drug dealers and drug gangs would no longer be able to sustain their organizations with drug profits and would decline markedly in activity, size, and ability to corrupt national institutions.

2. The United States could scrap the entire supply-side suppression effort to keep illicit drugs out of the country. The large expeditionary force of U.S. drug agents and military personnel could be removed from harm's way and returned home.

3. The cost of this War on Drugs (approximately $30- $40 billion annually for all branches of government) could be avoided.

4. Tax revenues on the sale of decriminalized drugs would offset the costs of drug prevention and treatment programs. Drug addicts who would become unable to function in society would pay for their recovery, institutionalization, or incarceration with tax revenues from the drugs they have used.

5. The armed forces could revert to their rightful role. The use of the United States armed forces in drug operations reversed national policy under the Posse Comitatus Act prohibiting use of military forces in domestic law enforcement. As then Secretary of Defense Caspar Weinberger wrote in 1985, "Reliance on military forces to accomplish civilian tasks is detrimental to both military readiness and the democratic process."[19]

6. The United States could heal relationships with friendly nations that were alienated by the War on Drugs

7. The U.S. government would gain control over all drug commerce within its borders. A legal market in drugs would permit the government to regulate, restrict, and tax drugs to achieve the lowest consumption possible—something that is impossible under prohibition.

8. Competition would give the advantage to a legitimate drug industry. Illegal untaxed drugs could not profitably compete with legitimate manufacturers, so drug consumers would be assured of government-regulated purity and quality, at a fair market price. Illegal sales of drugs would be comparable to the tiny ratio of illegal to legal alcohol sales in today's market.

9. Legitimacy would eliminate the need for anyone to have to deal with the criminal element. Also, without the selling pressure from drug pushers, drug prevention and treatment programs would be more successful. (See a complete discussion in Chapter 5.)

Politicians are Intimidated by the Drug Problem.

The American public is so outraged by crime from drug trafficking on the nation's streets, and at the social distress caused by drug addicts, that they are demanding greater action. Drug prohibition has been like having a "tiger by the tail." Drug warriors in the enforcement bureaucracy have convinced political leaders that, if drugs are legalized, drug addictions would increase as much as ten fold. Elected officials are afraid to make a move for fear that they will worsen the problem. If they can keep the drug problem swinging in the air, they seem to be doing something. To convince the public that they are attacking the problem, political leaders initiate heavy-handed diplomatic actions and punitive prohibition enforcement drives that create sound and fury but produce no positive results.

Hearts were torn as America watched a tearful Carroll O'Connor, the popular actor, discuss on television the suicide death of his 32 year old son after a history of drug abuse. As any parent would be, he was angry at his son's "friend," who had supplied the drugs to Hugh O'Connor. The drug problem was up close and personal to Carroll O'Connor, who in a later interview, said that he couldn't stop rampant drug use on his own CBS show, In the Heat of the Night, in which Hugh was also featured. "I gathered together the heads of departments, and said, 'Boys, help me find out who's doing the using and who's doing the selling,' the actor said. I think they were laughing at me. As much to say, 'Are you asking us to do the impossible; are you asking us to clean up a drug problem that's all over America?' In a way, I suppose they had a right to laugh."[20]

Most Americans see their children, relatives, and friends as victims of the drug dealers, not as persons responsible for choosing or avoiding their own predicament. In their anguish, citizens call out to government representatives to do something to stop drug use and drug violence. Prohibition has created the worst of all worlds—higher drug addiction rates, more personal tragedies from drug abuse, plus crime, violence, and corruption from illegal drug trafficking. Americans have been conditioned by public officials to blame foreign drug traffickers, but who would we blame for the drug abuse in the nation if there were no drug dealers, and drug users could legally buy drugs at a pharmacy? We all would have to acknowledge that it is the individual's choice to be a user. Our efforts should focus on persuading or coercing that individual not to be a user. We also must recognize that most of today's drug problems are created by the government's enforcement policies.

The Gordian Knot.

The War on Drugs is so interwoven that, like the legendary Gordian Knot, it defies anyone to untie it. Yet the weapon is at hand, and in one stroke Congress can slice apart the Gordian Drug Knot with its ultimate weapon, *repeal of prohibition*.

There appears to be a political revolution in Congress, as it reexamines many long-time federal social programs. It will take no less a revolution, as well as determination, by Congress to overturn the present federal drug policy. A few short years ago there were only a few avant-garde reformers who would dare speak out for drug-policy reform. Recently the media are presenting discussions on this subject in the public forum, but it has yet to be debated in the legislative chambers. But changing public opinion is about to force a discussion of a less punitive federal drug policy.

5

THE DRUG CARTEL'S FIFTH COLUMN

"Fifth Column" is a term that originated with the rebel General Mola, when launching his attack on Madrid in the Spanish Civil War of 1936-39. A newspaper reporter asked which of his (four) columns would be the first to enter the city; his reply was, "The fifth column"—by which he meant the rebel sympathizers living in the besieged city within the loyalists' lines. It has come to mean any subversive faction that cooperates with a foreign country to undermine the position and power of the home state[1]. In the context of the War on Drugs, the drug cartel's fifth column is the domestic direct-selling entrepreneurs of illegal drugs who are spreading drug addiction. in the United States. This is one of the most subversive and highly motivated forces, ever, in any war, and the motivating factor is "Big Money," real or imagined.

The prominent role played by this multitude of drug dealers and pushers in promoting drug use among United States citizens has never been fully appreciated by the government's strategic planners in this drug war, or by the Drug Enforcement Administration (DEA). Most people are inclined to write drug merchants off as petty criminals in a grimy business. This picture is true when one is looking at most street pushers or drug gang members, yet a drug dealer could be anyone. Consider the overall effectiveness of this aggregation of drug gangs and individual entrepreneurs. They make up the most successful sales force in the history of the world—selling over $100 billion of illegal drugs each year. That is an achievement that any American corporation would envy. These salesmen come from every industry and profession in the country, with many gainfully employed and some having respected positions in the community. Of course, pushers or dealers can also be members of a motorcycle gang or a juvenile crime gang, usually found in the inner city, but they frequently appear on Main Street, Any City, U.S.A. What is even more astonishing is that the cartels do not have to recruit these salesmen, conduct any motivational training sessions, or provide employee benefit packages. Replacements are not hard to find—

there are two waiting for every opening. These drug-pushing entrepreneurs are the spark plugs of the illegal drug industry.

Full-time dealers easily find helpers. A member of the drug lords' fifth column is usually a fellow worker in the office, an acquaintance at the factory, or another student at school. He or she seldom appears as the sleazy petty criminal that we usually associate with drug pushers. The process of spreading addiction is described by Professor James Q. Wilson of UCLA: "Drug use spreads in the same way any fad or fashion spreads: somebody who is already a user urges his friends to try...." But these "friends" have the additional motivation of pulling that person into the drug subculture and generating a new customer.

No American corporation can match, or even come close to the coverage achieved by these independent, direct-sell, drug entrepreneurs, who have infiltrated into every facet of our population. For instance, a writer for New York magazine in 1990 reported that the city's estimated drug sales totaled $12 billion, compared with $7 billion for all restaurants and bars.[v] Dealers and pushers are everywhere, from the halls of Congress to a bicycle shop in Peoria. Are these salesmen effective? You bet! Can we stamp them out? Not entirely. Not as long as there are fantastic profits to be made and a market exists for their product.

In China, authorities executed 27 heroin and opium dealers and destroyed tons of opium and heroin on just one day, June 26, 1992[vi]. It was not an isolated event in this totalitarian country—a total police state—run by one of the most ruthless regimes in the world. The penalty for drug use or trafficking in China is death, yet drug use continues to be a troublesome problem. Most Islamic nations also impose the death penalty for dealing in drugs, yet they have to periodically execute people for this crime. Even the totalitarian countries are not drug-free, as many people will risk life itself, if the price is right.

I Wanna be Rich

An interesting article appeared in The Miami Herald on Sunday, July 21, 1991, reporting on an Amway reunion on Miami Beach. It is instructive to compare this legitimate enterprise with the illicit drug trade:

> Motivational training mixed Saturday with high-powered salesmanship. The hustle of a business convention blended with

the bustle of a huge family gathering of 5,000. And a revival-meeting fervor flavored it all.

Most Amway distributors buy goods from distributors higher up in the Amway chain. Typically, they use some of the products themselves and sell the rest either to retail customers, or distributors they "sponsor" farther down the line. Distributors can earn bonus money if they sell enough products... The process can generate serious money.

The reunion presents speakers offering business advice and motivational exhortations. Also, audio tapes are for sale.... One music cassette was titled "This Dream Was Meant For Me." A song on the tape: "I Wanna Be Rich."

Whether you are an Amway salesman or a drug pusher, the theme song is, "I Wanna Be Rich." Amway is proof that a pyramid sales organization that continually builds down can create a mighty base, and provide some individual participants with fantastic financial rewards. Amway has built its legitimate organization with due diligence and considerable business acumen, emulating such direct-selling successes as Fuller Brushes, Realsilk Hosiery, and Tupperware. Amway is a highly respected corporation, and in no way is it suggested that the operation is illegal or unethical. The point is that the illegal drug business is structured in a similar manner, and whether the business is legal or illegal, a pyramid sales organization is a highly potent force. It is doubtful that the drug lords were as deliberate as the founders of Amway, but the illegal drug-selling business evolved that way and the outcome is highly successful.

In actuality few drug pushers get rich, just as few direct-sales distributors "make it big." But the lure of big money is there, as it has been with gold rushes, land booms, and speculative fever throughout history. In an illuminating 1990 article entitled "Coke Inc. Inside the Big Business of Drugs," Michael Stone contrasts a New Jersey drug boss with most street dealers. The former is the founder of "Basedballs," (crack packaged in red-topped vials) which cleared an estimated $20 million a year after eight years in business. But a boss like this permits his street dealers to keep only a small percentage of the large sums they take in. Consequently: "After factoring in the long hours, they come out a couple of dollars ahead of the minimum wage," according to anthropologist Philippe Bourgois.[4]

The Drug Cartel's Fifth Column

Bigtime drug dealers know how to recruit armies of pushers with the promise of easy money—plus excitement and "fun." For one thing, the bosses are ruthless. For another, they have an estimated "10 times as much money to work with as do those attempting to stop them," according to James Ostrowski, a legal authority. Finally, as Ostrowski says, "Drug enforcement suffers from all the inefficiencies of bureaucracies, while dealers are entrepreneurs, unrestrained by arbitrary bureaucratic rules and procedures."[5]

Drug dealers cannot use television or the print media to advertise and promote their products. Amway, Mary Kay, Avon, and many other direct-marketing firms, have already demonstrated that a network of individual entrepreneurs make an extremely effective sale force without advertising, and are an efficient distribution system for any product. Many drug users become pushers, usually to support their habit. Conversely, most dealers become users because of their familiarity with the drug they are handling. While they do not advertise, they do promote by word-of-mouth and personal testimonies. A user turned pusher will encourage his friends on social occasions to join him in a little "party," with the pusher supplying the dope. In this way he creates more users and gains customers.

The drug dealers possess a highly proficient, ingenious, and well-motivated sales force that creates markets where none existed before. Whether they entered the business for monetary gain, or started selling to finance their own drug habit, they frequently arrive at the same position of being a user and a dealer. What more logical way to increase your income, than to expand your customer base. Add to that a drug user's missionary zeal to convert his circle of acquaintances to his or her surrealistic world of psychoactive drug pleasures, and you have a very potent team of proselyters for drug use. Make no mistake about it—this is a difficult force to overcome when trying to reduce drug use within a population.

A quick end to violence on our streets

As the Federal, state, and local law enforcement agencies increase their efforts to stamp out drug supplies on our streets, the drug dealers push back ever harder. In recent years we have seen other foreign elements cooperating with the Colombian drug cartels, and sometimes competing with them. At various times and places we have seen the appearance and rise in power of the Jamaican posses, the Dominicans,

Chinese tongs, Korean gangs, and Vietnamese gangs. These foreign drug gangs must create new markets, or muscle-in on the local ethnic and black gangs that have been around for decades, thereby creating turf wars that lead to gang shoot-outs. All of these groups have the personnel and the money to match whatever force is thrown at them, and regardless of how many of their troops fall, they have recruits waiting to enlist. These foreign gangs are the source of many illegal immigrants, as well as gang members that travel back and forth on tourist visas between their homeland and the United States. These gangs must be ruthless or they won't survive, and they will stop at nothing to protect their enterprise. Should we give up the effort to rid ourselves of drug dealers? Not at all, but there is a quicker and more thorough way to put these people out of business.

Before we delve into the strategy to eliminate the drug dealers and the drug pushers, let us review our progress to this point in the search for a drug control solution, and note how this proposed action fits with earlier moves:

> Chapter 2 was a journey through this nation's history of drug use and the government's efforts to control addictive drugs. It was legal before World War I to import, manufacture, sell, advertise, and promote narcotics and cocaine in the private sector of the market. There were few restrictions by states, and none by the federal government, yet narcotics and cocaine were less abused during that period than today.

> Chapter 3 focused on the reasons the United States government decided on drug prohibition in the newly acquired Philippine Islands, and how the State Department coerced the Congress into passing domestic drug control legislation to support their international treaty initiatives. After prohibition in 1920, the United States had the dichotomy of increased drug use after each escalation in punitive anti-drug laws.

> Chapter 4 dealt with the drug cartels and the War on Drugs overseas by comparing it to other foreign wars, particularly Vietnam. It was demonstrated that the best weapon the United States has against the international drug syndicates is the repeal of drug prohibition, and the return of all drugs to the legitimate private sector.

To stop drug-dealing on our neighborhood streets, what quicker and more thorough way is there than for Congress and the states to follow through with the privatization of the legal retail distribution system for all drugs? The repeal of drug prohibition would follow the alcohol model. There is no recourse for the illegal drug pushers—they would be effectively eliminated from the drug market. Illegal drug dealers cannot profitably compete with legitimate drug manufacturers and pharmacy retailers, anymore than bootleggers were able to competed against legitimate distillers after the repeal of Prohibition.

Many persons with whom the author discussed the legal selling of cocaine and heroin in pharmacies were absolutely horrified at the thought. This reaction is strictly emotional and not reasoned when one considers that millions of dollars in illegal drug sales are taking place in America today and everyday. It should be self-evident that a legal drug market will sweep the drug dealers and gangs off the streets. The reader should save his or her concerns as to the workability of the plan until completing the book. Every concern will be discussed in light of this nation's experience with substance abuse and with the objective of reducing drug use under a legal system to the lowest possible level. But there should be no question that a legal drug market in the private sector will eliminate the crime and violence from currently illegal drug trafficking.

Evidence in favor of repealing drug prohibition has been presented in earlier chapters. The emphasis here is on the cost of the law-enforcement approach. It is high cost—low returns. A startling admission was made by Jack Lawn, the chief of the Drug Enforcement Administration in 1970: "Our enforcement efforts will continue to build statistics and fill prisons, but they won't turn around America's love affair with drugs."[6]

Even if we should achieve any success in reducing the supply of drugs with our present methods, we will forever be forced to maintain an extremely high-level law enforcement effort. Have we not seen with our own eyes drug dealers who willingly risk death every day? If not death from law enforcement officials, then, most certainly, death from rival drug dealers. As long as we create the environment for a lucrative illegal enterprise there will be crooks available to take advantage of it. We have created a climate where even the normally law abiding citizen is tempted to get involved in an illegal scheme, because the monetary rewards are so great if he succeeds just once.

Many readers have witnessed high-speed chases of law enforcement officers after drug operators, or have seen federal drug agents in an airport slam a suspect against a wall and arrest him with guns drawn.

The Enemy Is Us

Less than a mile from the author's home, in the Dadeland Shopping Mall, near Miami, shoppers were terrorized as a group of Colombian cocaine cowboys executed some of their rivals in a noon-time shoot out, firing hundreds of rounds with machine guns. A similar event—this time with law-enforcers involved—was reported in a Miami newspaper: "Shoppers at the International Mall had to duck for cover Wednesday evening during a brief gun battle between undercover police and drug suspects...."[7] Milton Friedman reasons that "the violence is due to prohibition and nothing else. How much violence is there surrounding the alcohol trade? There's some, only because we prohibit the sale of alcohol to children, which we should do, and there is some because we impose very high taxes on alcohol and, as a result, there is some incentive for bootlegging. But there is no other violence around it."[8]

The United States is so caught up in waging its War on Drugs, that Americans have forgotten why narcotics and cocaine were prohibited. America's GIs had their expression for situations like this: "When you're up to your a-- in alligators, it's hard to remember that your original intent was to drain the swamp." The intent of drug prohibition was to eliminate drug use—not to fight a bloody war. But, after seventy-five years of prohibition drug use is more prevalent and street violence more prolific. It is obvious that our strategy has not worked, primarily because many Americans have chosen to flout the law, as they did with alcohol. The good citizens of the United States do not have to put up with this kind of violence in our neighborhoods every day. We can achieve our objective without these senseless shootings and without the cost in money, lives, and the corruption. This lawlessness is undermining the best efforts of the Americans who want to reduce drug use in our society.

The situation is exactly the same as that encountered when the nation inaugurated alcohol prohibition. Just because Congress passed a law forbidding it, drinkers showed no intention of giving up their booze. Consequently the United States changed tactics, repealed that prohibition, and has since tried to reduce alcohol abuse by regulation, education, and firm persuasion. There has been no clamor from the American public to return to alcohol prohibition as a cure for the nation's alcohol problem. Yes, there is still an alcohol problem, but not an alcohol plus a crime problem.

There has been more than 20 years of get-tough law enforcement since the Nixon administration launched this War on Drugs in 1972.

The Drug Cartel's Fifth Column

President Carter carried on the policy, only to kick up the paraquat flap, when American DEA personnel sprayed that herbicide on Mexican marijuana fields. Mexican drug dealers harvested the infected crop anyway and sold it in the United States, causing a large number of marijuana users to become sick. The Reagan administration really got serious and gave then Vice President Bush the status of Drug Czar, with control over all government agencies participating in the drug war. At the beginning of President Bush's term of office, his administration went into an even more aggressive prosecution of the drug war.

Law enforcement has yet to solve anything in the drug war. Our prisons are overflowing with drug dealers, drug users, and crooked public employees; yet the supply of drugs on the streets has never been greater. In their zeal to get the drug dealers, the government's drug warriors have already resorted to seizure of private property without due process under the RICO Act. A federal appeals court ruled against the practice of seizing a defendant's property in a civil court proceeding if the defendant is also being prosecuted in criminal court, which is double jeopardy in the eyes of the court. The government was invited by the court to pursue the same seizures in criminal court, where prosecutors must prove "beyond a reasonable doubt" that the property was either used to commit the crime or bought with the proceeds. However, law enforcement agencies have preferred civil procedures, in which the government does not have to meet this strict burden of proof that the Constitution demands for the protection of the individual. After having lost in the review by the full court, the Clinton administration is considering an appeal to the U.S. Supreme Court.[9]

There is no stronger argument for reducing the authoritarian power of federal law enforcement than this assault on the Constitutional liberties of American citizens. The American public has acquiesced to this infringement by government on individual liberties because the RICO Act is aimed at drug criminals. These measures do not go far enough for the authoritarian government officials who believe that they know what is best for America and the individual citizen. The law enforcement agencies of the federal government bend the Constitution to better "protect" citizens from drug criminals. These drug criminals, like the violators of the old Volstead Act, are the creation of prohibition—a law designed to protect drunks from their lack of will power. This author would prefer to work with drug users to prevent or overcome their addiction than to endure the "protection" of the drug warriors. The next

71

step in this escalating use of law enforcement is the declaration of martial law.

William J. Bennett, the former Drug Czar of the United States, was the leading advocate for the Bush Administration's stiff-necked approach to cure this country's drug problem by creating an ever larger criminal justice system. In his speech before the Harvard University Kennedy School of Government, on December 11, 1989, entitled "Mopping Up After the Legalizers,"[10] he tried to make a point for more law enforcement by stating:

> Let me tell you that law enforcement does work and why it must work. Several weeks ago I was in Wichita, Kansas, talking to a teen-age boy who is now in his fourth treatment program. Every time he had finished a previous round of treatment, he found himself back on the streets, surrounded by the same cheap dope and tough hustlers who had gotten him started in the first place. He was tempted, he was pressured, and he gave in. Virtually any expert on drug treatment will tell you that, for most people, no therapy in the world can fight temptation on that scale. As long as drugs are found on any street corner, no amount of treatment, no amount of education can finally stand against them. Yes, we need drug treatment and drug education. But drug treatment, and drug education need law enforcement. And that's why our strategy calls for a bigger criminal justice system: as a form of drug prevention.

Mr. Bennett makes my point for me. No therapy or education program can be successful trying to work against such a network of drug hustlers. Returning heroin and cocaine to the private sector of the legitimate market would take the dealers and pushers off the streets, out of the offices, out of the factories, out of the colleges and universities, and most importantly, out of the schools. Right now, the nation's inadequate education and rehabilitation programs, are swimming upstream against the current of a diabolical and very effective drug sales force.

What ever happened to Mr. Bennett's 1989 program to clear drugs from the streets of Washington, D.C.? He has been silent on this subject because the Drug Czar could not clean up even a ten-square-mile area of this nation with law enforcement backed by the full resources of the federal government. Except for a few users thrown in jail, law enforcement failed to prevent one iota of drug use in the District of

The Drug Cartel's Fifth Column

Columbia. The irony of the situation is that Bill Bennett has espoused excellent plans for the prevention and treatment of drug abuse, but those plans are confounded by the very law enforcement approach to drug control that he embraces. The author's hope is that Mr. Bennett will reconsider his law-enforcement approach and join this crusade to develop a market-mechanism strategy for drug control in the U.S.

There is a ground swell developing in this country to take back some of the power that citizens relinquished to the federal government during the Great Depression, and through the period of the Great Society, when the people turned to the federal government for solutions. Mr. Bennett is one of the leaders in this movement with his organization Empower America, which he co-chairs with former congressman Jack Kemp. There is a dichotomy here, as Mr. Bennett eschews federal government solutions to the social problems of welfare and education, but embraces the epitome of an authoritarian government organization that would impose a law-and-order solution on a problem of public health. This author admires William Bennett's political leadership and the objectives of Empower America, but fails to understand the inconsistency of his position on drug prohibition, especially after the program has had decades of failure. Mr. Bennett should recall Professor Friedman's admonition that such a system will not work, and that if we are to end this War on Drugs, a market mechanism must replace the present authoritarian organization. With that basic concept in mind, let us employ the American way—free enterprise—to rid ourselves of these drug dealers and the entire drug subculture.

Legal narcotics and cocaine are the normal way.

Why do so many people react to legal drug sales as if it were an outrageous proposition? Some readers undoubtedly believe that the entire population of United States would be strung out on dope if pharmacies sold heroin, cocaine, and marijuana, legally and openly. But look back at history. Until 1920 a free drug market was the way it was and had been throughout the history of this nation. No historian would describe the United States in the first two decades of this century as a nation of junkies. Drug addicts were looked upon with shame and generally scorned as persons weak in character and lacking will power. Recreational drug use was not as widespread as today. For the most part, drugs were used for medicinal purposes. Alcohol was the recreational drug of choice and drunkards were considered the greater threat to social decorum.

For those who had trouble breaking their dependency, family doctors would help them through their ordeals. Treating addiction was a medical problem, and most addicts were under care of their physicians to keep their dosages under control and to monitor their general health. Most addicts could and did lead productive lives in spite of their addiction. Neither they nor their physicians were treated as criminals. This situation occurred at a time in the nation's history that is considered one of America's most moral, progressive, and productive periods.

For the first five years after passage of the 1914 Harrison Act, legal sales of psychoactive drugs were by prescription only. Exposure of a few flagrant "dope doctors" was one pretext for total prohibition. Before the mid-1960s in Britain, physicians were allowed to prescribe heroin for addicts. In the stormy Sixties a medical black market erupted among a few unscrupulous doctors. (One prescribed 600,000 heroin tablets in a year.) The British solution was to require physicians to send addicts to government-operated clinics for their heroin.[11] The proposed American free enterprise solution rejects government subsidy of addiction, but would permit the addict to buy his or her drugs in the legitimate market from a licensed pharmacist without the need for someone's permission. This places the responsibility for choosing to use drugs on the individual, and effectively eliminates any unscrupulous dope doctors, all street dealers and peddlers, as well as the need for an enforcement bureaucracy.

Panic caused by prohibition psychology has resulted in under-use of pain-controlling drugs, according to numerous authorities. "Society's failure to distinguish between the emotionally disturbed addict and the psychologically healthy pain sufferer has affected every segment of the population," according to Ronald Melzack, director of the Montreal Pain Clinic. "It doesn't mean you're addicted because you need more [pain-relieving medication]," says oncologist Paul Coluzzi of California's City of Hope. "What makes a drug illegal or legal has nothing to do with the drug. It's social convention," says John D. Loeser, director of the University of Washington's Pain Center. Finally, the U.S. Agency for Health Care Policy, in its guidelines for cancer-pain management, admits that the War on Drugs has intimidated doctors, nurses, and patients about using the most effective pain-controlling drugs.[12] Even the use of psychoactive drugs in pain-killing research has been discouraged or stopped. Research on the use of marijuana to relieve suffering from glaucoma and AIDS has been severely limited. For example, Donald Abrams, clinical professor at the University of California Medical Center, has struggled for two and a half years to win federal approval to test the effect of marijuana on patients wasting away from AIDS.[13] Reputable medical schools, hospital, and clinics certainly can be trusted to use addictive drugs responsibly.

Had our government leaders stopped short of prohibition in regulating alcohol and drugs, we could have been spared the decades of violence and corruption that followed our attempts to enforce prohibition after 1920. One can only admire our nation for the moralistic atmosphere in the country during the early part of this century. The goal of that society was noble. One cannot fault the nation for trying to eliminate the anguish and heartache of alcoholism and drug addiction by the simple step of prohibition. What if it had worked? Without the benefit of hindsight, a majority of Americans today would probably favor a prohibition experiment. But we do have the benefit of hindsight. While there may not be a solution to eliminating all recreational drug use, examination of the present drug control strategy reveals basic faults, that, when corrected, will improve the present situation.

K.I.S.S.

After passing out test booklets to a new class of enlistees, many military instructors would step to the blackboard and write, K.I.S.S. Invariably, one of the uninitiated would raise his hand to ask, "What does kiss mean?" With the all-knowing look that all instructors seem to have, he would answer in a loud tone, "KEEP IT SIMPLE STUPID." In other words, do not read something into the problem that is not there, and keep your answers straight to the point. One can become very discouraged when studying the proposed solutions to our drug problem that flow from our political and social leaders. The proposed solutions range from, "shoot all drug users," to, "set up government centers to give out drugs to all addicts." But as has been said earlier, no one could have come up with a more convoluted plan for drug control then drug prohibition—especially with the Justice Department attempting to enforce it by having drug agents running around the world stomping out drug crops, or shooting it out with drug dealers on neighborhood streets.

A study of the history of drug control, this nation's experience with alcohol prohibition, and this nation's success in reducing smoking, all reveal actions that are applicable to reducing recreational drug use in the U.S. The first thing to consider when devising a drug strategy is to keep it simple and within the normal economy. An authoritarian organization controlling drugs from the top of government has been a disaster, so it is time to return to the market based mechanism of pre-prohibition days. The ratio of drug users was lower than today, plus the nation has since gained valuable experience with addictive substances that can lead the United States to the lowest addiction rate of our history. A legal drug market, with thoughtful regulation, offers the best opportunity to reduce drug abuse to manageable levels and to eliminate the crime, killings, and corruption.

After the repeal of drug prohibition, the authority to determine and regulate the method of distribution would probably revert to the states, as it did for alcohol in 1933. Some states might opt for government operated drug outlets, but as mentioned earlier, some states are reconsidering their state operated liquor stores and privatizing them, so this may not be the wisest choice. The United States has already in place a most efficient pharmaceutical distribution system, and it would be folly to create an artificial system for the distribution and control of recreational drugs. Most states would probably use privately-operated, licensed, pharmacies, as they do now for prescription drugs. There have been many suggested avenues for retailing these drug sales, but the licensed pharmacist is suggested as the most efficient and logical choice since the market mechanisms are in place. There are also additional advantages:

- There is a pharmacist to serve every community.
- Licensed pharmacists are already state regulated.
- Pharmacists are educated and responsible professionals.
- Pharmacists are skilled in handling potent prescription drugs.
- Pharmacists would have the most to lose for violations—such as a sale to a minor.
- Legalization would place responsibility on the individual.

The individual can be educated, cautioned, and warned about the consequences of drug use. Warning labels can be placed on all drug packages, including the ultimate warning that use can result in immediate death. Under legalization, a person contemplating or already involved in drug use would have the family doctor, community drug clinics, and the pharmacist as sources of information and advice.

The Drug Cartel's Fifth Column

Discussions of the effects and dangers of any kind of drug use could be professional, open, and frank, and not restricted to the experiences and guidance of street peddlers. But, ultimately, the individual would be responsible for his or her choices and the consequences thereof.

It would be the same responsibility that the individual has today in choosing to smoke or not to smoke, to drink or not to drink. Should a decision to smoke, drink, or take drugs result in harm to person or property, then he or she is unconditionally responsible for the harm done. Being under the influence of a substance should not be a defense to escape just punishment or to avoid paying reparations. Any adult over twenty-one should be able to purchase marijuana, cocaine, crack, heroin, or any other FDA-certified recreational drug from a licensed pharmacist, without a prescription. Total access to adults should be given with a minimum of restrictions—the same freedom available in today's illegal market. The most important regulation should be a ban against sales of any drugs to minors, like the existing bans on sales of liquor and tobacco products to children (see Chapter 6). The nation's purpose should be to try to continually reduce drug use in a legal market, as it is doing today for tobacco and alcohol. Should a person have any questions about using a drug, there will be qualified people to advise him and possibly to dissuade him from using this substance. At the very least, legalization would take the user out of the criminal community and place him in contact with legitimate health and medical providers.

No advocate of legalization is so naive as to believe that some drugs would not find their way into the hands of minors, but most children can buy them today on their school grounds. Those sellers of underground drugs will quickly fade away—just as bootleggers disappeared after the repeal of alcohol prohibition. Maybe Bill Bennett's teen-age addict, cited in his speech, could then be helped without the pressure from street hustlers working against rehabilitation efforts.

At what risk do we repeal prohibition?

Let us remember that when we had unrestricted sale of cocaine, heroin, morphine, and opium, earlier in this century, no catastrophe occurred, nor did a drug crisis exist before prohibition was instituted. In spite of freely available drugs in a legal drug market there was no "crime problem" to compare to today's situation, and the ratio of drug addicts in that population was declining. From our review of history we have seen that drug prohibition resulted from actions by the prohibition zealots in an authoritarian organization—the Internal Revenue Service—trying to save the addict from himself. Professor Friedman weighs in with these comments:

> Should we have learned a lesson from Prohibition? When Prohibition was enacted in 1920, Billy Sunday, the noted evangelist and leading crusader against Demon Rum, greeted it as follows: "The reign of tears is over. The slums will soon be only a memory. We will turn our prisons into factories and our jails into storehouses and corncribs. Men will walk upright now, women will smile, and the children will laugh. Hell will be forever for rent." We know now how tragically wrong he was. New prisons and jails had to be built to house the criminals spawned by converting the drinking of spirits into a crime against the state. Prohibition undermined respect for the law, corrupted the minions of the law, and created a decadent moral climate—and in the end did not stop the consumption of alcohol.
>
> Despite this tragic object lesson, we seem bent on repeating precisely the same mistake in handling drugs. There is no disagreement about some of the facts. Excessive drinking of alcohol harms the drinker; excessive smoking of cigarettes harms the smoker; excessive use of drugs harms the drug user. As among the three, awful as it is to make such comparisons, there is little doubt that smoking and drinking kill far more people than the use of drugs....
>
> ...The ethical question is whether we have the right to use the machinery of government to prevent individuals from drinking, smoking, or using drugs....Fortunately, we do not have to resolve the ethical issue to agree on policy because the answer to whether government action can prevent addiction is so clear. Prohibition—whether of drinking, smoking, or using drugs—is an attempted cure that in our judgment makes matters worse both for the addict and for the rest of us.[14]

Experience demonstrates that the repeal of drug prohibition will results in fewer restrictions to commerce. Americans tend to overlook the strain and expense anti-drug laws place on normal commerce. Banks are burdened with regulations and reporting requirements to detect drug money laundering. The airlines have similar problems with their crews and baggage handlers being corrupted. Goods can not flow through our ports without the delays and expense caused by examination of cargo for contraband drugs. Weapon restrictions and gun regulations in the past thirty years are a direct result of the War on Drugs. Every crack-down by government officials on the movement of goods or people in the prosecution of the drug war infringes on our liberties and creates inconvenience to the public

When the U.S. Congress repealed alcohol prohibition in 1933, the American people took it in stride. It was a relief to get prohibition behind them. The prohibitionists and the bootleggers were unhappy about it. Many people liked prohibition, because they never saw a saloon and they felt better not knowing about the drinking. On the other hand, the attitude of the author's mother and father was that as long as people were going to drink, they might better do it openly. They preferred to deal with the problem above board, rather than having the cheating and hypocrisy of an illegal market. Many citizens shared this preference. Yet the policy being followed with illicit drugs has taken its toll on both nation and society. The violence, the defiance of the drug gangs, the bribery, the overloaded court calendars, and the corruption have almost destroyed our criminal justice institutions. Illegal drugs have caused fear and turmoil in the everyday life of most citizens. To speak editorially: Let's get it behind us, so we can concentrate on making a better society for all.

"Better an end with horror, than a horror without end"

The Reverend Robert Schuller, of the Crystal Cathedral in California, was interviewing the renowned psychiatrist Dr. Viktor Frankl, when he asked, "How did you develop your Logo Therapy technique?"

Dr. Frankl: I learned over time. I learned from Freud and Adler and so forth, but mainly from my patients.

In 1929 I was a student of medicine. But I was allowed to treat patients independently without any supervision at the university clinic. I remember once there was a patient who had spent many years lying on an analytical couch for psychoanalysis, being treated by hypnosis and so forth with no therapeutic effect. It was a case of agoraphobia—the fear of being in open places, suffering from the fear that he might collapse, faint, have a stroke or something else.

We have a saying in Austria, "I prefer an end with horror, instead of a horror without end." So I told this man, "Instead of year-long suffering from phobias, what about trying to collapse, to faint, to have a stroke on the street? Instead of being anxious about what will happen if you leave your home, leave your home with the strict intention: "I am going to collapse, to faint, to have a stroke and so forth." For a few seconds he went out to collapse and have a stroke, and at that moment he was free. A week later I asked the patient, "How are you today?" And he said, "Excellent." I asked him, "What did you do to be so excellent?" I always remember what the patient told me, but I scarcely remember what I told him before. And he said, "Doctor, you yourself told me I should leave my home with strict intentions..." So, I learned my own Logo Therapy. [15]

Here the author must editorialize again! It is time for Americans to apply a little Logo Therapy to their phobia about drugs. Drugs are not the masters of our fate. Drugs have no magical power to enslave our people. They can only enslave those individuals that choose to allow themselves to become slaves to a habit. We have the God-given power to make our choices in life, and we have thrust upon us the <u>consequences</u> of our behavior or actions, delivered either by the Almighty, by our government, or by our fellow man. Our government tried to take the individual's responsibility from him by prohibiting the use of narcotics or cocaine. Many Americans, however, chose to make their own decision on the use of drugs, thereby setting up the confrontation between the drug user and his government. This opened the way for the drug smuggler to establish his lucrative business.

During this War on Drugs the American public has developed a phobia about the repeal of prohibition. We have to be like Dr. Frankl's patient and take that first step, expecting that the worst will happen to us. Let us expect that we will get a tremendous increase in drug addicts in our society by legalizing drugs. Once we have made that step, we will be cured of our phobia. Then, to our joy, we will find that our worst fears were for naught. Some "experts" predict legalization will result in a huge increase in recreational drug use, and others estimate that it might result in a small initial increase, but this is mere speculation, for there is no evidence that supports either of these predictions. To the contrary, evidence from the period of legal cocaine and narcotics in this country points toward lower recreational drug use. Best of all, in return for a small risk, we will have lifted the burden of crime, violence, corruption, and hypocrisy from our society.

At last we will have freed ourselves of this horror without end.

6

OUR CHILDREN—
Mercenaries of the Drug Dealers

The War on Drugs has been an experience for the children of the X—generation like none ever experienced by any other generation in the U.S.A. Americans explain the pitfalls of addiction and encourage their children to avoid the use of drugs, but many juveniles choose to enlist in this war on the side of the drug dealers and pushers. Not only have they sided with the underworld, they serve in the front ranks of the drug sellers. Dreams of easy money have attracted thousands of teenagers, and there was even an arrest in New York City of a ten-year-old peddling crack cocaine. Tampa authorities detained a nine-year-old recently having $300-worth of cocaine in the school room of the Dale Mabry Elementary School. These are not isolated incidents, but are an all too common occurrence in the world of the drug subculture. A Time magazine correspondent gives a vivid summary: "Twelve-year-olds are working for eighteen-year-old dealers, who roam the streets with Uzi carbines."[1]

In reading the literature from the last century and the first decade of this century, one finds articles by public individuals expressing outrage over vendors and druggists selling cocaine to school children. A nickel then could buy two grains of cocaine.[2] However, it is evident from reading the literature of the period that juvenile recreational drug use was not the widespread problem that we have today. In most states, cocaine and heroin sales to minors were legal, since these substances were common remedies for certain ailments. They were not sold for recreational use, although many people used them for that purpose. The drugs were heavily advertised, and not restricted, yet crime resulting from drug use was insignificant in the turn-of-the-century society. Most so called drug-related crimes occurred coincidentally with criminals using drugs. The physiological effects of drugs rarely cause people to commit crimes.

Student drug sellers in today's schools seduce their classmates into experimenting with all kinds of substances that promise them a world of excitement and rich emotions. The seller's immediate motivation is money and a new recruit is also a potential long-term customer. But for the experimenter the thrill is short-lived. Frequently the youngster experiences a gut-wrenching and degrading slide into drug dependency that brings the additional burden of an expensive habit. While trying to achieve that higher plane of consciousness that the drug culture and the drug gurus of this nation have described to them, many youths destroy their character and personality, and throw away the opportunity for a fulfilling life. In the end, their drug experience turns to ashes. Parents must then retrieve the shell that remains, and try to restore their son or daughter to some form of respectability.

During the prohibition of alcohol America seldom saw teenagers, let alone preteens, involved in the distribution and selling of liquor. To be sure, many youths—especially college students—indulged in drinking forbidden alcoholic beverages.[iii] But they were not involved with the bootleggers, either as pushers or dealers. The drug war has gone on for so long and has deteriorated to the point that juvenile gangs are now heavily involved in drug activities, with drug-gang members in open rebellion against legal authorities.

Juvenile gangs and drugs—An unholy alliance

Some American youngsters have taken to the illegal drug enterprise like ducklings to water. Drug dealers recruit and train teenagers, and even preteens, to help in the drug trade by offering them outrageous amounts of money. The illegal drug business is an activity made to order for juveniles. It didn't take long for the drug dealers to recognize that kids could operate in this business quite effectively. Children seem to allay the suspicions of the authorities as they go about their activities, and should they be apprehended, minors are seldom punished or incarcerated. Unfortunately the kids are resourceful and adept at this business.

Tom Brokaw, on the nightly news, September 23, 1994, documented the spread of juvenile drug gangs from large cities, such as Los Angeles, to small towns all across the nation.[iv] Organizers from the Bloods, the Crips, or other gangs arrive in small towns, set up drug operations, and begin to recruit local youths. These new salesmen often realize instant wealth by pushing marijuana, cocaine, and heroin to their acquaintances in local workplaces and schools. Suddenly the town has an explosion in drug use on its hands and a proliferation of drug gang activities. The mean streets of LA and Chicago have been transported to small towns like Ardmore, OK, or Big Springs, TX. The drug problem in these towns will remain as long as illegal drug sales are profitable.

To those youths in the drug culture, the drug dealers have become role models, particularly to the minority youths in the ghettos. The young people see who has the money, sporty cars, and fancy women. There is excitement and daring in evading the law that makes these kids feel tough, smart, and important. Many of these drug-peddling juveniles make more money than any of the hard working adults in their neighborhood. It's hard to say "no to drugs" when, as the song says, "There is money for nothing and the chicks are free."

The U.S.A. has seen a steady increase in juvenile gangs dealing in illegal drugs during the past twenty years. They have become progressively more violent and heavily armed, and have assumed an ever increasing share of the task of transporting and distributing drugs. Their ability to operate effectively in the "mean streets" environment is the sustaining factor in their growing wealth, power, and prominence in the drug underworld. Fourteen years seems to be an average starting age for gang members, but to find preteens running with some of the most vicious gangs is not uncommon. Neighborhood gangs have existed for many decades in the large urban areas of this nation, but the new phenomenon is the wealth, the heavy firepower used by these kids, the number of killings, and the wide ranging activity of some gangs. The drug business frequently takes members out of their home towns and across state lines to transport drugs or to recruit sellers. The juvenile crime rate more than doubled between 1960 and 1990, while the teenage homicide rate more than tripled.[5]

It is difficult to penetrate juvenile gangs, since the members—except a few recruiters—all grew up in the same neighborhood and are wary of outsiders. Drug dealers like to work with these youths, because their identity with the gang makes it unlikely that the dealers are doing business with undercover narcotics officers. It is an unholy, symbiotic relationship, and illegal drug profits are the glue that holds the relationship together.

This amoral relationship between juveniles and drug dealers is one of the most destructive social situations ever experienced by the American nation. The wealth from the drug trade empowers many teenagers to declare their independence from any kind of parental control, to thumb their noses at the authorities, and to lead a life style of material excesses. It appears exciting to the juveniles involved, but with some bad experiences and more maturity, they realize they have pursued a self-destructing life style. It is a path leading to drug abuse, broken personal relationships, sexual diseases, long-term incarcerations, and often an early death. Juvenile gangs will continue to spread through our society like a malignant cancer as long as the promise of easy money lasts. Prohibition is the carcinogen that caused this cancer to develop. Repeal of drug prohibition is the chemo-therapy to put this disease into remission.

This is not to suggest that all juvenile gang activity would end with the legalization of today's illicit drugs, but legalization would deny drug sales as a source of income for the gangs. They would have to resort to more mundane and less lucrative crime to support their activities, and the big drug profits that empower these gangs will be gone. The end of illegal drug trafficking would certainly diminish the gangs' need for heavy fire power and would eliminate drug turf wars. The huge increase of weaponry in the hands of minors can be directly linked to juveniles involved in illicit drug activities. The Washington Heights neighborhood led New York City in murders in 1991, with 122, mostly drug-related.[6]

Since drug activities spill over into schools, guns have been used within the hallways of many schools, including some elementary schools. Drugs are not the cause of guns in the schools or crime on the streets. Rather, it is the Government's policy of drug prohibition. Initially, the U.S.A. followed the same policy in a battle against alcohol. Chapter 2 described the rise of gangs to control alcohol distribution in the Roaring Twenties. We also saw the decline of those gangs immediately after the repeal of alcohol prohibition. To be sure, many bootlegging gangsters of the 1920s went into "protection," pimping, gambling—or drugs. And the drug trade was where grown-up hoods recruited kids. Children are needlessly caught in the cross-fire of the drug war, and it is within citizens' power to stop this waste in human lives.

When does a minor become an adult?

There are two kinds of social analysis. One is the moral approach, favored by most conservatives. The other is the sociological approach, favored by most liberals. The moral approach advocates a Character

Our Children—Mercenaries of the Drug Dealers

Ethic, and compares existing behavior with a standard set by religious and ethical authorities. Stephen Covey in The Seven Habits of Highly Effective People, refers to "Character Ethic as the foundation of success—things like integrity, humility, fidelity, temperance, courage, justice, patience, industry, simplicity, modesty, and the Golden Rule. The Character Ethic [teaches] that there are basic principles of effective living, and people can only experience true success and enduring happiness as they learn and integrate these principles into their basic character."[7] The sociological approach examines how humans behave and considers possible incremental improvements. The perceived disadvantage of the sociological approach is that those who take it may settle for a low behavioral standard when facing difficult facts. Many liberals perceive a disadvantage to the moral approach in that it may result in a standard that cannot be reached because of stubborn facts. Although your author favors a moral approach, he will endeavor to acknowledge sociological objections as liberals interpret the facts opposing his preferred behavioral standard. In the remaining pages of this chapter, the author will present a moral standard while noting sociological objections.

Almost every hand would be raised if one asked a class of 4th graders, "How many of you can drive a car?" They think they can drive a car, but grown-ups know better. These children are a long way from having the maturity and judgment to operate an automobile. Being able to start the engine and manipulate the controls are not the same as being a qualified operator, but these children do not yet know the difference. It is the same for teenagers and 20-year-olds. They all believe that they are old enough and mature enough to handle, tobacco, alcohol, drugs, and sexual relationships. From the author's perspective, most persons below the age of 21 are not yet ready to make adult decisions, or to accept adult responsibilities—not without further development, training, and experience. Some juveniles are mature while still in their teens, and some adults are not mature at 40, but is it wise to rush the majority of adolescents into premature adulthood? I think not. The author's perspective gets implied support from an eminent sociologist, John S. Coleman, who takes this position: "In many traditional cultures, there is no adolescent period. Adolescents are ready to assume adult roles.... But in industrialized countries adult society does not have a place for teenagers, so they create a distinctive culture of their own...."[8] In the author's view, "teenage culture" extends to age 21 and is not yet adulthood.

Here the author feels a need to be autobiographical. My dad and mother made a pact with their four sons that, if they would not smoke until their 21st birthdays, each would receive a gold watch. From the perspective of a Depression-age kid, this was a magnificent reward. To give my sons a similar incentive in today's inflationary world, it cost my wife and me a new car for each, presented to them with pleasure on their 21st birthdays. The watches and the cars were significant incentives, of course, but they were more symbolic than significant, and not necessary to instill values in the child. My stronger incentive was to live up to my parents' expectations. Rewards gain a child's attention, but the building of character and discipline in the child by parents takes many years of training, instruction, and example. My parents' objective was to help me resist peer pressures to smoke until I was of an age to make a mature decision. By the time I was 21, I no longer felt a desire to mimic adult vices—I was secure in my own person.

Parental attention is the key factor. But, the social critic will say, three families in ten today are headed by single parents, usually employed.[9] Also, half of all women hold jobs.[10] A serious problem the author must admit, and a challenge to everyone. In many cases the role of parenting must be taken by grandparents and other relatives or by churches and civic groups. But, by whatever means, the nation must see these children educated, trained, and steeped in traditional values, which would take the nation's schools and community social institutions back to teaching and practicing the Character Ethic.

The 26th Amendment pressures the adolescent

During World War I and II, the United States turned to conscription to provide the needed personnel, as it had during the Civil War, to wage those two wars. Twenty-one was the age of majority and was the initial minimum age for the draft. However, as pressures built to increase the forces, Congress eventually lowered the draft age to 18. Interestingly, the minimum draft age during the Civil War stayed at 20, because of the high number of volunteers. In the eyes of the law, draftees under the age of 21 were minors, but the exigencies of national interest required that minors be inducted, trained, and sent to war. National pride rose from the way American boys conducted themselves in battle. Most people felt: "They went into the military as boys, but they came home men." The minimum draft age remained at 18 through the Cold War including the actions in Korea and Vietnam.

A large controversial question, as noted above, is when a young person should be treated as an adult—should reach so-called legal majority. In 1971 the passage of the 26th Amendment to the U.S. Constitution, extended the right to vote to all citizens over 18. From the beginning of the nation it had been 21. One argument for 18 as the age of majority is that millions of teenagers are in the workforce. Another argument is that millions of teenagers are married. But the argument that stampeded the national leaders and the state legislatures to pass the 26th Amendment was, "if a person is mature enough to fight or die for the nation, is not that person mature enough to vote?" Whatever the sociological evidence may be, there is obviously a moral judgment in defining adulthood on the basis of employment, marriage, or parenthood, but, in the opinion of the author, acting to change the age of majority in the emotion of the unpopular and bloody Vietnam War was not wise. Even after passage of the Amendment, opposition to conscription and the Vietnam War was so intense in 1972 that President Nixon took a calculated risk, stopped the draft, and went to all-volunteer armed forces. To the surprise of his critics, the all-volunteer service has worked well.

Military service should not automatically qualify young people as adults, in the author's view. Unquestionably such service requires increasing maturity, as well as courage and initiative. But the teenage recruit receives rigorous training to increase his or her self-reliance. Discipline is strict to insure that the soldier, sailor, marine, or airman (or woman) reacts almost instinctively to command. Unit integrity must be maintained. The esprit de corps of a unit is a substitute for parents and family. Most importantly, attention is focused on a specific objective— not the case in civilian life.

If military service cannot immediately transform adolescents into adults, modern American civilian life falls short to a much greater degree. Yet after 1971, along with right to vote, teenagers gained the right to drink alcohol in many places and to sign contracts and get loans. The immediate result was a sharp rise in teenage auto accidents, sexual encounters, pregnancies, and credit problems. Some officials at all levels of government have tried to restrict the activities of "adults" between 18 and 21 until they have gained greater maturity. Notably, Congress has raised the national drinking age, and some states are considering a high minimum age for the legal purchase of tobacco products. In 1992 the Director of the Centers for Disease Control urged states to set 19 as the minimum legal age for buying tobacco.[11] The author would urge 21 be set as the minimum age.

Congress establishes a minimum drinking age

A few years after passage of the 26th Amendment Congress established a uniform drinking age of twenty-one for the nation. The age was raised to control juvenile drinking and to reduce the number of minors dying in highway accidents resulting from drinking and driving. A federal drinking age was especially needed to stop minors from driving across state lines in pursuit of alcohol. This legislation was achieved by coercion rather than mandate. Congress simply refused to provide matching highway construction funds for those states that did not have such a law on their books.

"Zero-tolerance" laws, which penalize under-21 drinkers for driving after one drink, have been adopted by 23 states and the District of Columbia. Such laws subject young drivers with a blood-alcohol level of 0.02 percent to the same penalties as over-21 drivers who are legally drunk. Urging Congress to enact legislation pushing states to pass such laws, President Clinton said, "A blood-alcohol content of 0.02 percent— the equivalent of one beer, one wine cooler, or one shot of alcohol— should be enough to trigger the drunk-driving penalties for people under-21." Zero-tolerance laws are awaiting a governor's signature in Rhode Island and Connecticut. Thus half the states are on the verge of action against youthful slaughter on the avenues.

Older citizens have done a poor job in convincing young drinkers that one can get just as drunk on beer and wine as on hard liquor. Unfortunately the point of most student drinking is to get high. We have to convince them that you also lose control of your life when you are intoxicated. When one's judgment is impaired he or she is out of control, and many things can happen—all of which are bad. It can be anything from an unintended pregnancy to killing your best friend. Then there is the ultimate bad happening—throwing away your own life to experience a high. Regrettably many college students are binge drinkers.

Tighter laws for adolescents apparently have had a beneficial effect—along with education in schools, churches, and communities— according to a 1995 U.S. Public Health Service Program called "Healthy

Our Children—Mercenaries of the Drug Dealers

People." It found that there is less use of alcohol (as well as marijuana) among the young; that fewer young people are beginning to smoke; and that deaths from auto accidents are down.[12] But teenage pregnancies have increased, as has binge drinking among college students[13] The fact that government officials are now pulling back on the adult rights extended to teenagers in the passions of the Vietnam War era is demonstrative proof that the 26th Amendment to the Constitution was a mistake. If one needs further evidence, answer this question: "At what age should a person be permitted to purchase hard drugs when Congress repeals drug prohibition?"

Readers with an optimistic sociological outlook will emphasize the progress that has been made and simply call for increasing education. Those with a more conservative moral outlook, like the author, will applaud the progress and approve increased education, but will also urge a return to a pre-World War I definition of adulthood. Adolescents 18 to 20 are still children, and should not be shoved into adulthood; rather, they should be guided under parental supervision and direction until age 21.

Let the kids have a childhood

Although your author advocates a free market in drugs for adults, he also advocates banning drug sales to minors, as is generally accepted for alcohol and tobacco products. In a complex modern society, young persons should be considered children until the end of adolescence. American parents have consistently been pushing their children toward adult activities at an earlier and earlier age. While these children have been exposed to the tawdry side of life to a greater extent than other generations, through R-rated motion pictures and tabloid television, they are not more intelligent, better educated, or emotionally better equipped to handle life's responsibilities at an earlier age. Since the 1960s, America's youth have been granted more privileges, with less responsibility demanded of them, than any generation in our history. Living in a world of supersonic transportation and instant communications does not permit us to compress the childhood experience into fewer years. Maturity does not come from values communicated to the child by the media and entertainment industry; rather, maturity comes from the discipline imposed and the values imparted to the child by his or her parents—preferably, both parents.

The sociological obstacles to the two-parent home have been discussed earlier in this chapter, along with ways to overcome these obstacles.

Children function better and feel more secure in their lives, when they know the limits of acceptable behavior. Too many parents, even those of supposedly caring families, do not enforce the limits of acceptable behavior, or try to teach moral values. They do not realize the heavy burden they place on the juvenile when they leave the decision to the child to decide moral right or wrong. Many parents surrender their authority to surrogates, or yield to their children's demands, then live to regret it when the child falls into the abyss of the lost. Peer pressure from the drug world so overwhelms some children that the drug subculture lures the youth away from the family in spite of the parents' best effort.

A Nation's Responsibility

The 1990 Final Report of the National Commission on Drug-Free Schools has excellent recommendations for reducing drug use among our school children. [14] It is a comprehensive report prepared by a dedicated group of government officials and community leaders from across the nation. The Commission's Co-Chairmen were William J. Bennett and Lauro F. Cavazos. It recommends an all-out attack to prevent children from trying or using any drug, including alcohol and tobacco. The legislative proposals are bold and right on target. This attack on the demand-side of the drug problem would be an effective measure in reducing drug use among America's juvenile population. It includes tobacco and alcohol in the drug program, and recommends the restriction of advertising on both of these substances. What little progress the U.S.A. has made in reducing drug use results from prevention efforts.

Unfortunately, the report strongly opposes legalization of narcotics, cocaine, and marijuana—a position that keeps the nation deeply mired in the drug morass. More importantly, illegal drugs will continue to hamper the effectiveness of prevention programs because of the counter-actions by the drug subculture. The destructive effects of drug dealers and drug pushers on prevention and rehabilitation programs were highlighted in the previous chapter.

Our Children—Mercenaries of the Drug Dealers

The Commission, moreover, makes some assumptions about legalization that are just not supported by facts.[15]   Consider the following statements from the Report:

1. *If drugs were legalized, health care costs would increase dramatically to meet the needs of more drug users and addicts.*

Wrong!   Legalization of currently prohibited substances would reduce drug use as demonstrated by the nation's earlier experience with legal drugs, especially if done in the manner suggested by this book. This book's program for reducing drug use incorporates most of the recommendations from the above report, but recommends that these prevention programs be conducted in a legitimate drug environment. Furthermore, drug taxes paid by the drug-using population would fund prevention and treatment programs that are now borne by all taxpayers. America's experience with legal narcotics and cocaine during the first two decades of this century shows that the nation can reduce drug use in a legal drug market.   Remember, that one consequence of drug prohibition has been an increase in drug addictions.

2. *Legalization would not reduce crime, nor would it diminish the profit motive for most drug traffickers, because a criminal motive still would exist to undercut government-regulated prices and turn a better profit.*

That statement is ludicrous and without substantiation. The crime associated with alcohol prohibition faded away with legalization of that product. After repeal of alcohol prohibition, legitimate dealers did not have to secrete their activities from the police, or kill each other to protect their enterprise. Illegal liquor sales after repeal were an insignificant portion of total sales and of little concern to the authorities. It would be the same for illegal drugs. Pharmacists selling legal, FDA-certified psychoactive drugs over the counter are not going to indulge in crime, bribing officials, or hiring adolescents as look-outs. The Commission makes this statement without presenting facts or reasons for its conclusion.

3. *In addition, some national indicators show that drug use finally is decreasing for a significant percentage of young people, so it would be absurd public policy to change the legal status of these drugs.*

That statement sounds like something right out of the Vietnam War. Remember the statement repeated so often by the Johnson Administration, "There is light at the end of the tunnel." There has been no significant reduction in drug use since the post-prohibition nadir in

91

drug use reached in World War II. Since that time drug use increased dramatically with only a changing of preference from one "dope" to another. Would it have been absurd public policy to have changed the drug policy in the 1960s, a period that drug use raged out of control? We are not even <u>half way</u> back to the lower level of drug use that existed at the time the government imposed drug prohibition. There will be no progress toward reduction of drug use as long as we have an active sale force of underworld drug entrepreneurs pushing these drugs in our society. Any gains we may have made among adolescents come from our prevention programs and these programs will be far more effective in a legal environment.

The underworld drug culture must be destroyed

CBS's program "Sixty Minutes" May 2, 1993, showed the rampant drug smuggling and drug dealing still thriving into 1993, with no ability by the government's forces to stop it. The United States has lost control of its borders, with both drug smuggling and illegal aliens. A Time correspondent asks: "How can any military force secure the eighty-eight-thousand-mile perimeter of the United States?"[16] In the Sixty Minutes program, CBS was documenting young illegal aliens from the Dominican Republic, arriving in New York city without a dime in their pockets and making a thousand dollars selling drugs on the street the first week they were in the country. This is happening in every major U.S. city, only with different ethnic groups. What a country of opportunity! Only in America could this happen.

The foulness of the underworld drug culture that has permeated American society also envelops the nation's children. This evil force has to be removed before one can expect any lasting success from some of the good treatment programs now available. The hard-core juvenile drug operators have to be eliminated if these programs are to be effective. Drug use is spread and encouraged by those in the drug culture who profit from drug sales. Any juvenile completing a drug treatment program will find himself back among the wolves as soon as he returns to his old haunts. He was originally recruited by his acquaintances in the underground drug culture, and they have a vested interest in keeping him hooked

America had a large criminal element that sprang up with alcohol prohibition, but those gangs of hoodlums suffered a decline when the alcoholic beverage business reverted to legitimate interests after repeal. Many of those same gangsters resurfaced a few years later in the drug trade, but the big difference from the days of alcohol prohibition has been the large participation of juvenile gangs, beginning in the 1960s.

Prohibition attempts to deny the mature adult the responsibility for his own decision, but prohibition can protect the juvenile from having to make a decision for which he is not yet capable. The parents have to make many decisions for their children during their maturing years. With legalization of drugs, society would have to make the decision on when minors have reached an age of maturity that would allow them to make a reasoned choice as to the use of drugs. Congress has said that twenty-one is the age of maturity for drinking alcohol; accordingly, twenty-one should be the age for the use of drugs. If society requires youngsters to refrain from either of these substances until they are twenty-one, the probability is that most of them will have enough maturity and responsibility never to be abusers of either substance.

Adults have a special obligation to minors. Nothing angers most Americans more than an adult taking advantage of a child for the adult's purpose and pleasure. We have rigorous laws to try to prevent harm to juveniles; yet our children appear to be in harm's way more and more often. Many say that child abuse has not increased but that minors are now quicker to expose the perpetrators and the media more likely to report the story. The author's observation is that there is more abuse of children today and that it is the direct result of the growing number of live-in arrangements among unmarried adults with children, as well as more dysfunctional traditional families in the United States. The breakdown in family structure in the American nation is a subject that would fill several books. The decline of the family makes it all the more incumbent upon parents and other concerned adults to set an example with a drug-free environment.

There are good prevention programs available today. Mathea Falco describes some of them in her book *The Making of a Drug Free America—programs that work.* She points to two, Life Skills Training (LST), and Students Taught Awareness and Resistance (STAR), as being among the most effective programs in the country.[17] More than 250 alcohol and drug programs for adolescents are listed in a book by two child guidance experts, Reaves and Austin.[18] Such programs, launched in conjunction with a national campaign to change social attitudes about alcohol and drug use, have an even better chance for success. But all of these programs and campaigns are of no avail, unless the nation first has a sound basic policy governing drugs, as well as alcohol and tobacco.

The apple doesn't fall far from the tree

There are no cures for addiction. Once dried-out, clean, or sober, an addict cannot use the substances of his addiction on occasions without falling back into addiction. Abstinence is mandatory. This is the one program that is effective above all others, whether a person is genetically predisposed to addiction or not. Nancy Reagan called it "Just say No to drugs." She was ridiculed by some sophisticates for being too simplistic, but it is the most positive treatment for addiction, when applied one day at a time in a discipline like the Alcoholics Anonymous twelve-step program. A person who refrains from taking that first drink, smoke, or hit assures himself that he will never become addicted to any substance. If addicted, he can again become sober or clean by refraining one day at a time. Let the author expand on that thought with a true story.

The father was an alcoholic. A loving person when he was sober, a terror when drunk, which was the way he stayed for the better part of thirty years. His three lovely daughters were raised in the comfortable home of caring grandparents and their long-suffering mother, because Daddy could never hold a job for long. Their material needs were met and they received abundant love, care, and nurturing from the functioning adults in the home. Their father was always an embarrassment and a disturbing factor in the girls' lives, but still deeply loved by all of his daughters, who just wanted him to get "well."

The oldest girl—call her Georgianne—consciously feared becoming an alcoholic, because she felt that she was probably genetically predisposed to addiction. Georgianne developed a deep faith in God, which sustained her in the effort to avoid addiction. The two younger girls experimented with both drugs and alcohol in their teens and fell prey to dependency on both substances, in spite of their older sister's best efforts to help them avoid addiction.

The sisters were genetically similar. Their economic situation and environment were equal. They all had equal opportunity to take control of their lives. Each girl exercised her freedom to choose. One chose wisely, and has enjoyed the satisfaction and contentment that come with having a loving marriage and a stable family. The two younger sisters have struggled in turmoil all of their adult lives as a result of their substance abuse, and only now, in their middle years, have they been able to bring some semblance of order to their lives. The primary difference in the three sisters' approach to life was that Georgianne made a conscious decision to abstain during her teen years and had the support of her faith. This is also the guiding principle behind Alcoholics Anonymous that has made its twelve-step program such a success.

What are we trying teach?

"Ultimately the most important weapons in the War on Drugs are the least tangible ones; self-discipline, courage, support from the family, and faith in one's self. The answer is traditional values. And if we want to stop our kids from putting drugs in their bodies, we must first ensure that they have good ideas in their heads, and moral character in their hearts."—President George Bush, remarks in recognition of Drug-Free Schools program.

The importance of models in social learning has been demonstrated by leading psychologists such as Albert Bandura, Stanford professor and onetime president of the American Psychological Association.[19] Parents and family members are a child's chief models. Also important are neighbors, teachers, local merchants, and church and youth group leaders. The influence of other adults, however, should not be overlooked, even when youngsters' relations with them are quite indirect or only through the media. These others include business leaders, entertainers, legislators, athletes, and jurists. All adults are under an obligation to present themselves to rising generations as models of responsible behavior.

Responsibility in the modern world too often has given way to a "no-fault" attitude, resulting in a "blame game." All socially disapproved behavior is blamed on someone else or on circumstances. This attitude is applied to a range of behaviors from cheating in school to malingering on the job to high crimes including grand larceny, murder, and treason. The no-fault attitude is seen in Ivy League universities and service academies and at the highest levels of business and government. Is it any wonder that irresponsible sexual behavior, child neglect, shoplifting, welfare cheating, substance abuse, and drug peddling occur among the less-affluent, less-educated, and under-age members of American society?

Schools cannot fairly be given all the blame for the low state of American morals, but they surely deserve a share of the blame. How much blame is debatable, as are the questions of where and how far schools have gone off the right course. A conservative educator, William K. Kilpatrick of Boston College says, "many of today's young people have a difficult time seeing any moral dimension to their actions." His observation is substantiated by a liberal psychologist, Lawrence Kohlberg of Harvard, who finds that "adolescents inevitably see moral judgments as partly interpersonal."[20] Kilpatrick attributes the primary cause of this attitude to "a failed system of education that eschews teaching children the traditional moral values that bind Americans together as a society and a culture. That failed approach, called 'decision-making,' was introduced in schools 25 years ago. It tells children to decide for themselves what is right and what is wrong. It replaced 'character education.' Character education didn't ask children to reinvent the moral wheel; instead, it encouraged them to practice habits of courage, justice and self-control."[21] Stephen Covey ties up the package with his discernment that "the Character Ethic is based on the fundamental idea that there are principles that govern human effectiveness—natural laws in the human dimension that are just as real, just as unchanging and unarguably 'there' as laws such as gravity are in the physical dimension."[22]

Milton Friedman was a product of the New York Public School System. He believes he received an excellent education, but deplores the current state of the public schools in the United States. Professor Friedman says: "We all recognize that the War on Drugs is destroying our inner cities. But...the next most important factor is our defective educational system.... Both failures have the same source. The War on Drugs is a failure because it is a socialist enterprise. Our schools are deteriorating because it is a socialist enterprise. Except possibly for the military, education is the largest socialist enterprise in the United States...." [23] Friedman goes on to say: "I challenge you to find any major problem in the United States that you cannot trace back to the misuse of political mechanisms as opposed to market mechanisms."[24]

It is hoped that Congress will remove the authoritarian organizations that control the school system and the drug market, and return both enterprises to the people. Then, perhaps, Americans can rebuild their families; reclaim their children from the drug war; and be rid of the guns, crime, violence, hypocrisy, and corruption that are the by-products of the War on Drugs. No one has described the despairing picture of children caught-up in this insane world of illegal drugs as well as Terry Williams, an Afro-American sociologist who spent months hanging out with, and writing about, *The Cocaine Kids, The Inside Story of a Teenage Drug Ring.* Why drug prohibition must end is clear as Terry Williams completes his story of The Cocaine Kids:

Today, as I walk through this city of fallen dreams and unquenchable hope, to the neighborhood where I first met Max and the Kids, I see a new generation of Cocaine Kids in faded jeans and unlaced sneakers, draped with gold chains, their arrow-pointed haircuts topping fresh faces and hard frowns. These kids are grown before their time, wise before they leave home, smart before they go to school, worshippers before attending church, rule-breakers before they know the rules and law breakers after they know the law.

On the corner of 162nd Street, three boys and two girls shout to me almost in unison, their outstretched hands revealing their wares, "got that coke, got that crack, got red caps, got blues, got yellow ones—you choose. What you want, my friend? What you need?"

The innocence of the young is lost in Washington Heights these days as a new generation of street corner boys and girls enter the shadowy world of dealing and prostitution. A new generation of Cocaine Kids is embarking on a voyage, searching for dreams that most will never find.[25]

97

7

NEGOTIATING A PEACE IN THE DRUG WAR
Finding common ground for a new drug control policy

The status quo forces in America's War on Drugs have circled their wagons and are prepared to defend drug prohibition. In many cases their reputations and jobs depend on continuing the War on Drugs. It would be difficult to persuade this large cadre of law enforcers and bureaucrats that ending the drug war for a return to a legal drug market would be beneficial to the nation. They would have to accept the fact that their years of effort have been meaningless and that their careers are over as drug-war fighters.

The feelings of the drug warriors are familiar to the author, since he fought in a losing war in Vietnam. Few critics questioned the strategy of using United States forces as shooting participants in a war on behalf of the South Vietnamese. While the goal to stop the spread of communism and to establish democracy in that developing nation was a noble cause, Americans learned that freedom is not something you can give people. It must be won by the people of the nation concerned. The U.S. military saw more than fifty thousand of their compatriots fall in the Vietnamese effort, and in the end their sacrifice was in vain. The government's drug warriors are in a similar situation trying to make America drug-free. Only the American people can do that for themselves.

The innocence of our entry into Vietnam was not wholly unlike our entry into Prohibition. As one reads Frederick Lewis Allen's 1931 account of that time you are struck by the similar innocence of the American people to an impending tragedy:

> If in the year 1919...you had informed the average American citizen that prohibition was destined to furnish the most violently explosive public issue of the nineteen-twenties, he would probably have told you that you were crazy. If you had been able to sketch for him a picture of conditions as they were actually to be—rum-ships rolling in the sea outside the twelve-mile limit and transferring their cargoes of whisky by night to fast cabin cruisers, beer-running trucks being hijacked on the

interurban boulevards by bandits with Thompson sub-machine guns, illicit stills turning out alcohol by the carload, the fashionable dinner party beginning with contraband cocktails as a matter of course, ladies and gentlemen undergoing scrutiny from behind the curtained grill of the speakeasy, and Alphonse Capone, multi-millionaire master of the Chicago bootleggers, driving through the streets in an armor-plated car with bulletproof windows—the innocent citizen's jaw would have dropped.[1]

Would the writers of the Harrison Act of 1914, have voted for its passage if they could have somehow foreseen where their action would lead the United States in 1996? And knowing what it brought, can the United States continue with drug prohibition? The United States Government must be realistic in designing a new drug policy. "[David Musto] points out that Americans have often twisted themselves out of shape, early in the century and today, to avoid 'the painful and awkward realization that the use of dangerous drugs may be an integral part of American Society.' The refusal to deal with this issue is reflected even in the text of the Anti-Drug Abuse Act of 1988, which sets as the government's goal a drug-free America by 1995."[2] Not only was it an unrealistic goal, but in 1996 the drug problem is bigger and more expensive than ever. No one doubts the sincerity and determination of the drug prohibition advocates. Most among them believe with all their hearts that, with more effort on their part and greater support from the public, the war on drugs is winnable. Like our military in Vietnam, they blame their lack of success on their detractors and the failure of the home-front population to support them. But the reason for their failure is that they, like the military in Vietnam before them, labor under a <u>flawed</u> strategy and are doomed to fight an endless war with mounting casualties.

Before launching the final push to install a new national drug strategy, the forces for a workable-drug-control-policy must neutralize the barriers to change erected by the advocates of status quo. The latter's position is threatened because their strategy has failed, but even though they enter negotiations from a point of weakness, they appear determined to bulldoze their opposition. Those of us who favor change will try to persuade our fellow citizens on the status quo side to join us in attacking drug use with a new strategy. If Americans can have a rational discussion of our national drug control policy without rancor, accusations, and hysteria, this nation can develop a new strategy that will reduce drug use and relieve the distress from illegal drug trafficking.

Building social barriers against addictive drugs

At the end of the last century, the United States faced a growing problem of dependency on narcotics, cocaine, and alcohol. Although addicts were comparatively few, their numbers were increasing. Everyone used opiates in the nineteenth century, either prescribed by their physician or self-administered in patent medicines. The medical profession was slow to recognize the addictive power of these drugs. Physicians and patients alike used these substances with little concern as to the long-range consequences. By the end of the nineteenth century, there was already a growing concern and rising public intolerance toward narcotics and cocaine abuse. With the introduction of aspirin in 1899, physicians finally had a nonhabit-forming painkiller for all but the most serious needs. The first decade of the twentieth century saw a decline in the use of addictive substances, particularly after the passage of the Food and Drug Act, of 1906, with its labeling requirements.

"As the number of addicts declined, the size of the smaller, urban male lower-class addict population remained steady, but the group became far more conspicuous. People began to see addicts as lowlifes. This would have a vast impact on the newly set precedent for federal action on policies to control habit-forming drugs."[3] A strong social disapproval arose against the casual use of addictive drugs, even while narcotics and cocaine remained legal. In short, information and education were succeeding. With addictive drug use in decline and the drug users under pressure from society to shape up, there was little enthusiasm in the nation or in the Congress for prohibition of these substances.

The pressure for domestic narcotic controls came first from the State Department. The reader will recall from earlier chapters that the interest of the State Department in domestic narcotic controls stemmed from our efforts to enforce an opium ban in the Philippines. Opium smuggling had quickly become a problem in the Archipelago and the strategy chosen to stop it was to destroy drug crops and stop opium trafficking in source nations. Unfortunately this strategy requires the cooperation of many nations. Domestic narcotics control legislation was passed at the insistence of the State Department to demonstrate this nation's dedication to achieving an international agreement on control of the opium trade. It gave the United States high moral ground on which to take leadership of the International Opium Conference. Their noble goal was for the world to eliminate, or greatly reduce, the use of narcotics for any purpose other than medical. Obviously, the International Opium Conference, and the follow-on agreements of the United Nations, have failed to achieve that goal.

Does legalization imply government tolerance of drug use?

Mark S. Gold, and Mathea Falco are among several authors who have written recent books on treating and preventing drug dependency in this country.[4] Both Gold and Falco adamantly oppose drug legalization and believe that legalization would lead to increased drug use. Falco states that legalization would signal a fundamental change in American attitudes, implying tolerance rather than disapproval of drug use. Almost every supporter of drug prohibition uses the argument that "legalizing these drugs sanctions their use," but nothing could be farther from the truth. Using drugs for any reasons other than medicine was highly intolerable to the American society in the first two decades of the twentieth-century. Listen to America's foremost historian on narcotic controls, David F. Musto, Professor of Psychiatry and the History of Medicine at the Yale School of Medicine:

> Passage of the Harrison Act came after consultation with the trade and professional interests concerned, from the obligation of America to other nations, and with the support of reform groups, but it was not a question of primary national interest. Although drugs later became a great popular issue, the passage of the Harrison Act in 1914 seemed a routine slap at a moral evil, something like the Mann Act [against prostitution] or the Anti-Lottery Acts.

In short, drug abuse was considered wrong, like prostitution or petty gambling, but not a big problem. Thus few citizens paid attention to the small cadre of reformers pushing for the prohibition of narcotics and cocaine. Dr. Musto continues:

> It went largely unnoticed because the question of controlling narcotics had none of the controversy associated with the prohibition of liquor. Perhaps half the nation saw nothing evil in moderate drinking. Most Americans described themselves as in

favor of temperance, which could be interpreted as being opposed to public drunkenness. But almost no one ever used the term temperance in discussing the use of opiates or cocaine after 1900; by the teens of this century both classes of drugs were deemed in public debate to have no value except as medicine. The closest a public spokesman would come to defending such drugs would be to say that they were not especially harmful as compared, say, with alcohol and with a vigorous effort in progress to outlaw alcohol, the description did not protect narcotics from criticism. By 1914 prominent newspapers, physicians, pharmacists, and congressmen believed opiates and cocaine predisposed habitués toward insanity and crime. They were widely seen as substances associated with foreigners or alien subgroups....[And] it was feared that use of all these drugs was spreading into the "higher classes." The only question publicly debated with reference to narcotics was how to control, not (as in the case of liquor) whether to control.[5]

How to control, not whether to control, addictive drugs is still the question today. The majority of citizens, if they held any opinion about narcotics and cocaine, linked them with underclasses, criminals, and the insane. Yet prohibition brings along a host of destructive social factors without accomplishing the designed purpose—a reduction in drug addictions. It has worsened the drug problem and comes with a heavy cost to fund enforcement. The author's conclusion: Drug prohibition, except for minors, should not be part of any policy to reduce drug use in this nation. Illegal drug trafficking is the major part of the drug problem, and it cannot exist with legal drugs where there is unrestricted access. A New Strategy is the only solution.

The New Strategy would be based on the private sector drug market of 1914, when America was successfully reducing drug addiction in that legal market before rushing into drug prohibition. The New Strategy recognizes the individual drug user as the enemy in the War on Drugs, and concentrates on preventing drug use. Adults should be left to make their own judgments on drug use, but drug users seeking help would be treated in community centers; addicts who ask for help would be admitted to drug rehabilitation hospitals; and incorrigible drug addicts who cannot care for themselves (or who have no family that will care for them) would be removed from society and placed in disciplinary camps until rehabilitated. Citizens would work to establish a national intolerance toward drug use and try to persuade each person to use common sense to avoid abuse and addiction. Can today's society do this? Certainly! Both alcohol and nicotine are legal, addictive drugs. The United States' massive public health program has educated and encouraged citizens to abstain, or restrict, their use of these substances. The government, together with educational and religious institutions, has successfully reduced cigarette smoking over the past 30 years and constantly urge moderation in use of alcohol with some success. Drug use can be reduced with the same methods.

Even some people who support legalization think that there could be an increase in drug use—particularly if the nation legalized all drugs and the free market was allowed to take its course. They reason that drug companies would replace the drug cartels and the drug dealers in pushing and promoting controlled substances. We have seen the aggressive actions taken by the tobacco and alcohol companies in pushing their addictive products. Drug companies presumably would do the same to obtain their "market share" of a legal drug market. Definite steps would have to be taken to minimize the risk of drug use encouraged by commercial advertising and promotion. Advertising and marketing of tobacco and alcohol products are controlled by a combination of legal controls and voluntary cooperation. Some brewers and distillers even promote moderation. Finally, it is surprisingly true that, even with legal drugs and aggressive advertising by drug companies before the Harrison Narcotic Act, the U.S.A. never reached today's high rate of drug addictions.

Reducing demand through education.

The need to control or restrict drugs is not questioned; only the wisdom of prohibiting drugs completely. Drug prohibition drove the narcotics and cocaine market underground and out of the control of government to regulate it. The American public has always had contempt for the drug addict and the drug user, but fear of the drug addict in today's society stems more from crimes associated with the enforcement of drug laws than from actions by the addict himself.

Both Gold and Falco are among experts who believe that the U.S.A. is making good progress in dealing with the drug abusers that want to kick the habit. Both want the government to concentrate on reducing demand for drugs by providing programs for the prevention and treatment of the drug addict. They recommend spending less on supply-side suppression of drugs. Both have a good grasp of the demand-side of the equation. Falco aptly points out that European nations that practice toleration toward the drug user, and apply less-harsh criminal penalties, have a considerably smaller addict population than the United States. There may be other factors involved, but the comparative rate is a fairly consistent fact.[6]

These experts' recommendation to place emphasis on demand reduction is right on target, and this author supports their position as far as it goes. But demand reduction is only one-third of the program. Demand reduction offers no relief from the large number of incarcerations for prohibition crimes, including mere possession. Demand reduction offers no solution to the worldwide drug syndicates, or the drug-associated crime, corruption, and killings. As long as such experts insist on keeping psychoactive drugs illegal, drug trafficking will continue, and there will be no sales tax revenues to fund the good treatment and prevention programs they suggest. Furthermore, under prohibition, the recovering addicts in these rehabilitation programs are constantly being reclaimed by their "friends" in the drug subculture.

A successful program for teenage addicts, called Recovery High School, died recently in Albuquerque, NM, for lack of funds. The state legislature and city school board were unwilling to give adequate regular tax funds to Recovery High, and sufficient private donations could not be found. But a sales tax on addictive drugs could have saved this school with its slogan "Endings are New Beginnings."[7] Meanwhile a third of the treatment specialists will be laid off at the Center for Alcoholism, Substance Abuse, and Addiction of the University of New Mexico, because of a drop in funding. A five-year federal "seed grant" ran out, and the hard-pressed state government felt unable to make up the difference. A drug sales tax could have filled the gap.[8]

Prevention as well as rehabilitation programs are threatened with shortfalls in funding, in this era of budget-balancing and tax-cutting. A large revenue source could be tapped by the legalization of all drugs. Sales taxes on abused substances, moreover, would be an appropriate source of funds to combat substance abuse. Even the billions of dollars raised with drug taxes would be paltry compared to the saving of funds now expended on the War on Drugs at every level of government—local, state, and federal. An endangered program is UNITY (United Indian Tribal Youth), which circulates radio and print messages urging "tradition, not addiction." The messages are funded by the National Institute on Drug Abuse, a tax supported agency. A program using federal, foundation, and business funds is the National "Drugs Don't Work" Partnership (DDW). Created in 1993 by President Clinton's Drug Advisory Council, DDW received a three-year $800,000 grant from the Robert Wood Johnson Foundation in 1994. DDW's goal is to broaden the partnership from 10,000 to 80,000 companies in 10 states. An admirable goal, but what about the other 40 states and several hundred thousand companies? The Robert Wood Johnson Foundation also has made grants to several Indian tribes and to Atlanta's Mission of Hope, in order to stimulate drug-free workplaces. But there are hundreds of other tribes and cities. One foundation, even a great one, cannot do it all—especially with shrinking federal participation. Clearly drug taxes, and saved expenditures, that legalization would bring are urgently needed.[9]

There is a covert but free market today, for narcotics, cocaine, and marijuana. Anyone, including minors, can buy these illegal drugs at a freely negotiated price. Drugs are pushed and are more available in this illegal market than they would be in the legal, yet controlled, market proposed by the New Strategy. The illegal market comes to the customer on the streets or at the office or factory, and is available to minors in their schools and neighborhoods. Legalization would make these substances available only through legitimate businesses, who would pay taxes on their income and collect tax revenues for the government. The drug user would at least have to walk to a pharmacy to make his purchase, instead of having it delivered to his work place.

Mathea Falco, in particular, raises many legitimate concerns about how to handle certain aspects of legalization. Others have raised these objections, and the answers to Falco's questions are found in the analysis of empirical evidence from this nation's history. Falco acknowledges that the United States now has "the highest rate of addiction in our history, exceeding even that at the turn of the century, when opiates, cocaine, and marijuana were legally marketed."[10] That earlier society was actually reducing drug use while there was a free and open market for narcotics and cocaine. The United States today, on the other hand, has been losing ground with the law-and-order approach and at the same time has to contend with a huge and destructive criminal underworld. Falco states in her book, "We know that drug abuse is largely driven by demand, not supply." It follows then, that legalization will not necessarily increase drug use by making drugs available through legitimate rather than illegal channels. Illegal drugs are in great supply in the United States and are readily available from drug selling acquaintances working alongside of almost everyone.

You can't ignore the drug culture

There is a thriving drug culture, drug lifestyle, or drug business—whatever you care to call it—that perpetuates drug use by the members in that society. It is a society based on the sale and distribution of illegal drugs and pulls in all those who profit from it, those who use drugs, or those who can be persuaded to experiment with drugs. This underground culture attempts to <u>recruit every new member possible.</u> Once into drug use, people have to maintain their association with this group since it is the source of their drugs. In many cases, drugs are also the source of their income. Many persons, male and female, are drawn to this society in admiration of the free spending, flashy personalities of that community's leaders, the drug dealers. The same glamorization of the underworld occurred in the Roaring Twenties, when alcoholic beverages were illegal and bootleggers were lionized in many circles. Legalization would eliminate drug dealers and destroy the mystique of the drug culture.

Mathea Falco says, in stating her opposition to legalization, "The two most powerful reasons for recent declines in marijuana and cocaine use among educated, affluent Americans are health concerns and increasingly negative social attitudes about drugs. Holding on to these gains and extending them into high risk groups will require intensive prevention, education, and treatment campaigns. The drug laws play a critically important role in this effort by conveying social values and defining the limits of permissible behavior...."[11]

Let us consider her premise that "drug laws convey social values and define limits of permissible behavior." Societal attitudes convey values and define limits of permissible behavior, not laws. Laws are the result of societal attitudes. Just consider public attitudes toward either alcohol or drugs. The American society in the second decade of this century had already defined the limits of permissible behavior for both drugs and alcohol without any law. The majority in that society were so opposed to alcohol and addictive drugs that they passed laws banning them.

Negotiating a Peace in the Drug War

Thirteen years later that same society had developed contempt for alcohol prohibition and repealed that law to welcome back <u>legal</u> alcohol.

A 1995 article in New York magazine describes today's upper-income drug culture in that city and its suburbs. Responding to the article, a young recovering addict wrote to the editor: "I started using heroin because people like William S. Burroughs write about it so glamorously....But no singer, writer, or film, told me how devastating the drug truly is."[12] Compare Frederick Lewis Allen's description of the booze culture in the Roaring Twenties: "This overwhelming flood of outlaw liquor introduced into the American scene a series of picturesque if unedifying phenomena: hip flasks uptilted above faces both masculine and feminine at the big football games; the speakeasy, equipped with a regular old-fashioned bar...; well-born damsels with one foot on the brass rail, tossing off martinis;...the sales manager serving lavish drinks to the visiting buyers...."[13]

Many in the society of the 1960s suddenly became very tolerant and receptive to psychoactive drug use, even though the U.S.A. had drug prohibition laws on the books, backed by strong law enforcement. Again, social attitudes prevailed over law as a conveyor of values and as a definer of permissible behavior. Social disapproval and ostracism of users are more effective than drug laws in discouraging drug use. Today's society has failed to control its drug problem with ever more harsh laws. Before there were any drug laws, American society conveyed its social values by raising social intolerance for drug users and by insisting on individual responsibility for one's actions. Permissible behavior was defined by the shame cast upon any habitual user, or by social ostracism for anyone who allowed himself to fall victim to addiction.

We should also look to the success the United States is having in discouraging the use of tobacco—not by punitive smoking laws, but with education, publicized health concerns, and public intolerance of smoking in social settings. Falco's premise in dealing with people in high-risk groups is also discounted. They are a rebellious minority that has <u>already</u> rejected society's value of law, and they prefer to define their own limits of permissible behavior. They must be shocked out of their self-destructive ways, like the young New Yorker quoted above. Until you break down this impermeable drug society, it is difficult to educate, or reason, with individuals in this culture.

If we were to legalize all recreational, psychoactive drugs, we would have eliminated the mystique of the drug culture and its secret dealings. The treatment and rehabilitation centers could then deal with individual drug users without interference from drug gangs and dealers trying to influence the patient. Programs of prevention, treatment, and potential cures would have a chance to get through to the individual without the addict hiding behind the shield and protection of the drug society. If drugs were legal, drug peddlers would not exist and there would be no incentive to interfere with a person going for treatment, since the addict would be no longer a drug dealer's employee, customer, or supplier for someone else.

Conservatives and the free market

Legalization of psychoactive drugs has become such an emotional issue—and therefore so irrational—that conservatives and liberals are lined up on both sides of the issue. On the thinner side of legalization are such stalwart conservatives as William F. Buckley, Jr., Milton Friedman, and George Shultz; while opposing legalization are equally conservative William Bennett and Jack Kemp. President Clinton's former Surgeon General Joycelyn Elders offended other liberals, as well as conservatives, by advocating legalization. Neither the liberal Carter administration nor the conservative Reagan administration advocated legalization.

One might suppose that all conservatives would favor a free market in drugs, a minimum of government intervention, and a reliance on individual self-control. Similarly, one might suppose that all liberals would oppose a rigid "law-and-order" approach in favor of "social engineering" to reduce drug use and rescue addicts. Yet psychoactive drugs have been so demonized—in the manner of pre-Prohibition "Demon Rum"—that politicians need rare courage to advocate legalization. The public has been so conditioned by the drug-war bureaucrats that it believes legalization is a "catch-word" for the "promotion of drug use." Even as one of the most powerful House Speakers this century, Newt Gingrich found it necessary to use tough language condemning drug users and traffickers to couch the suggestion that legalization might be an option if prohibition enforcement doesn't work.[14]

Negotiating a Peace in the Drug War

The best way the U.S.A. can reduce the scourge of drug abuse is to encourage a return to traditional American values and to create a strong social intolerance of psychoactive drug use within a legal drug economy—just as Americans are doing with alcohol and tobacco.

Death to drug addicts

Ed Koch, former Democratic Mayor of New York City, advocated execution of all drug dealers. Some Americans think death for all addicts would not be too severe a punishment. In 1958, the United States passed a drug law that called for death to anyone causing the addiction of a minor, but no one was ever executed under that law. However, many nations execute people for possession of even small amounts of drugs. The small island nation of Singapore has mandatory death sentences for drug offenses and over the past 20 years has executed 78 offenders. In September of 1994, Singapore executed the first westerner for a narcotic crime—a Dutch businessman carrying 9.4 pounds of heroin. A few years ago two Australians were executed in neighboring Malaysia for bringing marijuana into the country. Many other Asian nations also have the death penalty for drug crimes.

China does not release figures on executions in that nation for drug offenses, but on occasion will announce executions, such as the one day when it executed 27 persons for drug offenses. The significant point is that nations that execute for drug offenses have totalitarian or authoritarian governments. To even consider capital punishment for a consensual crime is not consistent with the character of the United States, where personal freedom is cherished. It is not a viable option in a free society. Neither is prohibition, where a government bureaucracy determines one's personal choices—even if one's personal choices are unwise.

Varied approaches to drug control

Leniency. The Dutch policy toward drugs is at the other end of the scale. Officially neither production, trade, nor consumption of drugs is legal in Holland. Unofficially the police choose to look the other way unless drug trafficking is too obvious or too prolific. The Dutch attitude: Keep it small and not too intrusive—then drug consumption will be ignored. Of course the legal definition is a fraud—not legal, but permitted. The Dutch authorities feel it is the right policy for them. In their opinion their drug problem is now well managed, except for the annoyance caused by some drug tourists. When the rest of Europe relaxes its drug policies, the Dutch feel that the drug tourist problem will go away

Prescription Dispensing. In 1924 Britain adopted a policy of permitting physicians to prescribe morphine or heroin to their patients including addicts. Physicians and pharmacists were required to record dispensed drugs. Although a tiny black market existed in London for "weekend users," addiction declined between 1924 and 1960. In the Sixties, when drug tourists started to come to the United Kingdom, some physicians gave them prescriptions or even sold drugs on the black market. Hence a new policy was adopted in 1966. Under the new policy, heroin may be prescribed only in a limited number of clinics, although morphine and methadone may be prescribed by any physician. Addiction in Britain is again declining, and it now appears that the increase in the 1960s was exaggerated. Sweden and Denmark also permit doctors' prescriptions of opiates to addicts.[15]

Decriminalization. Used in the context of drug policy, decriminalization is a broad term that often encompasses a range of measures such as removal of criminal sanctions for simple possession of drugs or lowering of penalties for possession of small amounts of illegal drugs.[16] Drug possession in small amounts was recently legalized by a ruling of Colombia's Supreme Court, while trafficking and production remain illegal. Decriminalization is a contradiction. You cannot have something half legal and half illegal. Even if a person is committing no crime in consuming a drug, a crime had to be committed to provide him with it. A few of our States have decriminalized possession of small amounts of marijuana. While they have succeeded in relaxing the atmosphere between police and the drug users, it is hypocritical at best. Decriminalization does not appear to be an honest or a logical answer to America's drug problem.

Free Distribution. Switzerland's government approved the free distribution of hard drugs to 700 addicts on June 24, 1993, in a three and a half year experiment to help that nation decide whether to legalize consumption and dealing of hard drugs.[17] You can expect that experiment to be a failure, in the opinion of the author. Switzerland's government is making a mistake by subsidizing the drug addict with free drugs. Government-provided free drugs, except in a drug treatment facility, should have no place in a U.S. private-sector legal drug market. Charles Murray made the point in his book *Losing Ground* that, whatever a government subsidizes, the experience has been that there will be an over-abundance of that item—be it pigs, cheese, illegitimate children, or drug addicts. In the new strategy the addict can buy his own drugs on the economy. If he resorts to crime to obtain drugs, then he should be incarcerated for the crime, not his drug habit. Involuntary treatment for addiction should be imposed on all criminals in confinement, although it is not likely to be successful unless an addict wants to become clean of drugs.

Teach the Unwise, Don't Make Criminals of Them

Drug use, whether it leads to addiction or not, is <u>unwise</u>. Some call it foolish or even stupid, but drug use should not be a crime, or the user imprisoned—unless the action of the person under the influence harms, or has the potential to harm, someone else. The Old Testament Book of Proverbs put it like this: "Wine is a mocker, strong drink is raging: and whosoever is deceived thereby is not wise."[18] There is no prohibition of alcohol by the Judeo-Christian Bible, but it admonishes every person to exercise good judgment and moderation in its use. Some become over-zealous in their allegiance to prohibition and are quick to condemn use of any substance that they consider harmful. We see that happening today, as Congress debates the regulation of tobacco. Some are calling for a ban on all tobacco products. But the prohibitionist's attitude is best illustrated by the following anecdote.

A Protestant Minister found himself seated next to a Catholic Priest in an airplane flying coast to coast. A friendly conversation began and rapidly developed into a warm ecumenical relationship as they discussed the relative merits of their service to the Lord. After awhile, their discussion was interrupted by a flight attendant with the drink cart and a cheery question, "Would you gentlemen care for a cocktail, beer, or wine?"

The Minister replied rather indignantly, "Alcohol never touches my lips."

He was shocked to hear the Priest say, "I believe I will have a glass of wine."

As the Priest sat sipping his wine, the Minister became more and more agitated and finally, unable to contain himself any longer, he blurted out, "Father, I am surprised that you, a man of the cloth, would drink alcohol in this plane, in clear view of all these people. What kind of an example are you setting?"

"Oh," said the Priest. "I would remind you, Reverend, that our Lord and Savior was known to partake of the fruit of the vine."

The Minister sat silently for several moments, with jaws tightened and his neck growing red. He finally turned to the Priest and said, "Yes, I know he did, but I would have thought a whole lot better of him if he hadn't."

If we incarcerate everyone for unwise or stupid behavior, we will all serve time occasionally. A person may smoke cigarettes and even get drunk, both of which actions are unwise behavior, but not criminal. If that person were to fill his gas tank while smoking, or to drive his automobile while drunk, he would have committed an act that should be punished. It is the same with dope. Using it for recreational purposes is unwise and foolish, but should not be criminal.

A famous American surgeon, William Halsted of Johns Hopkins University, became severely addicted to cocaine in 1884--an addiction which led to his temporary disability, hospitalization, and a year of recovery in the Caribbean. Although his recovery from cocaine addiction resulted in a lifelong addiction to morphine, he was still able to return to a productive and brilliant career until his death in 1922.[19] One should hasten to add that his productivity was in spite of his addiction, not because of it. In today's climate he would probably have lost his license to practice medicine, but in Halsted's time drugs were legal. Also, his experimentation with drugs was legitimate research, but it still cost him a lifetime of addiction.

The anti-legalizers make a litany of charges against legalization that just does not hold up under close scrutiny. One of their claims is that relying on taxes from legal drugs would place the government in the intolerable position of benefiting financially from drug addiction. Yet almost everyone seems eager to tax the equally dangerous addicting drugs of nicotine and alcohol. Would you leave the drug revenues to the drug dealers and overseas drug lords, so they can continue to push for more users and create more addicts? Or would you rather that the government use the tax revenues paid by drug users for the benefit of programs that prevent or treat addiction? Another argument is that drug laws discourage first-time users because they do not know how or where to buy illegal drugs, yet practically every first-time user is given the drug by a friend or acquaintance. But the primary reason for the repeal of prohibition is that our present policy of drug prohibition just is not working. Every objection to legalization can be refuted by looking back to that time when drugs were legal and using our own experience as a guide.

Teddy Roosevelt ascended to the Presidency in 1901 and became one of our most forceful and active chief executives, raising the United States to the status of a world power. He also symbolized the Progressive Era, when government action was considered the best way to solve problems. Progressives and the reformers that followed were sure that they could make this a better world by the simple action of banning alcohol and drugs. Surprisingly tobacco would not be recognized as a <u>major health hazard of the nation</u> for another 63 years. But now we have the wisdom of hindsight and the experience of four generations. We can all see that prohibition has not and is not working in our society, so let us drop the idea of banning tobacco products and think about lifting the drug ban. It is time to discuss placing all the addictive psychoactive drugs in a legitimate market under one regulatory policy for alcohol, nicotine, narcotics, cocaine, marijuana, and all designer drugs. The only way to remove the criminal element from the illicit drug trade is to go "Back to the Future." Our future lies in taking the underworld out of the drug trade and returning the manufacture, distribution, and sale of all drugs to legitimate businesses. This was the way the drug business operated before March 1, 1915, when the Harrison Narcotics Act became law. The method we use to regulate and control tobacco or alcohol use in this nation seems a proper and correct basis to establish a drug control policy.

Drinking an alcoholic beverage is legal, but a Northwest Airlines crew was recently sentenced to prison for drinking before a flight. The government did not have to prove that they were intoxicated, only that they had been drinking within the twelve hours before the flight. Even a <u>slight</u> impairment of an air crew while operating an aircraft can have disastrous consequences. Similar rules apply to train and boat crews and truck drivers. Regulating behavior for the safety and health of its citizens is a government obligation. Prohibiting an individual from deciding what he or she wants to eat, drink, smoke, or inject is government intrusion. Government's efforts to bring information on life's hazards and risks to the attention of its populace, or trying to persuade individuals to live a lifestyle that enhances a healthier and happier society, is a government activity to be encouraged.

Liability of drug users after legalization

Let us look at improper behavior while under the influence of alcohol, narcotics, cocaine, marijuana, or any other recreational drug. Everyone must understand that the very decision to take a substance that can alter your judgment, behavior, mood, or mind makes you liable and responsible for any harm or damages you do while under the influence of a substance. To plead innocent to a crime because "I was crazy on drugs" is no defense. Such an offender should pay the full penalty under the law for his or her actions.

The United States Supreme Court has declared addiction a disease, but that decision is certainly arguable. Long before addiction occurs, character and responsibility come into play. It is difficult to feel sorry for those who become addicted, since they cannot help knowing that the substances they were casually using could result in a tragic consequence. To say that a person has a gene defect, or is an addictive personality, is a poor excuse for becoming addicted to tobacco, alcohol, or drugs. Everyone is in full control of his actions and behavior before he takes the first drink, injection, or puff, so let's attack the problem by teaching abstinence from substances that can do you no good. Remember, there is no cure for addiction—abstinence is the only effective treatment over a lifetime.

The Supreme Court's decision to label addiction as a disease has had the most tragic consequence. It has forced the federal government to support alcoholics and drug addicts on the streets with SSI disability payments from the Social Security Administration.[20] It is misplaced compassion at best, and these cash payments feed the addiction, not the person. Alcoholics and addicts living on the streets should be treated in an institution or work camp under supervision until they are able to care for themselves. Uncle Sam has become an "enabler" for thousands of dope addicts and alcoholics with a self-inflicted condition, which is controllable with abstention but is consciously perpetuated by the individual. The decision that labeled addiction a disease should be challenged and changed.

Let us also consider an employer's right to refuse employment because of substance use (the term use, instead of abuse, is purposely used). An employer should have the right to determine what drugs, and the amount of use, he is willing to tolerate in his employees. The mere fact that substances are legal should not give an individual the right to use harmful substances that hamper his ability to do his job and then demand the "right" to employment.

There is precedent for such policies. Many municipal fire departments have refused to hire smokers, since fire-fighters that develop lung disease invariably blame it on the occupation rather than the more probable cause, smoking. Smoking has a direct impact on the health insurance premiums that a corporation has to pay for its employees' group health plan. Employers should be able to legally discriminate against applicants if they have a history of drug use, or if drug use is revealed in their physical examination for employment. Life and casualty insurance companies would certainly rate the premiums higher for substance users. Such discriminatory actions against drug users are persuaders for people not to use drugs.

Drug legalization and sports

Athletic leagues and conferences should not have to modify their policies on substance abuse because of legalization. Alcohol is a legal drug, but alcohol abuse brings quick retribution to any athlete. NFL Commissioner Paul Tagliabue decided to view the abuse of alcohol in the same punitive light as drugs and steroids.[21] A prime reason for barring drug use on sports teams is the large investment that teams have in their players and the damage that drugs do to a player's performance. Unfortunately there are some notable examples of sport stars whose performance deteriorated dramatically after they become involved with psychoactive drugs. Professional sports particularly demand strict mental concentration to maintain maximum performance, and the lack of total concentration can result in mental mistakes that cause a Pro-Bowl or an All-Star player to look like a rookie. Many legal drugs and steroids are banned as performance-enhancing substances, as would be a stimulant drug like cocaine. There is no reason that anything should change in a sport's drug policy because of legalization.

The Enemy Is Us

Goals of a New Drug Strategy

If one takes the time to look, even a casual observer could see that prohibition set the United States on a bloody, crime-ridden, and costly drug nightmare that created more addicts, crime, and violence than the U.S.A. can tolerate. One of the nation's first objectives after the repeal of drug prohibition should be to collect tax revenues on the sale of these FDA-certified drugs to cover the social costs to our communities and the health costs of addicts. Federal, state, and local governments should tax these substances approximately as liquor is taxed, but not to such an extent as to increase the price to the point that it creates a black market.

With legalization, we would replace the local drug pushers with the licensed pharmacist, who would not be trying to push substances to build up his clientele. Also, he would not be likely to engage in a shoot-out with his nearest competitor. He would not hire children as lookouts for the police, or to deliver his drugs. It would be wonderful to have the drug mess off our streets. Then our police could concentrate on crimes against persons or property instead of knocking over crack-houses or busting dealers

The author has tried to persuade the defenders of the status quo that their objections to the legalization of drugs are not as well founded as they might have believed. There is still their major objection to drug legalization to be considered and discussed—fear of increased drug use. If the status quo defenders insist on keeping narcotics and cocaine illegal, drug prohibition and the War on Drugs will become the object of an ideological battle to be fought in the political arena.

Prohibition is an authoritarian system controlled by government from the top, and it has failed. The strategy is flawed and that system cannot be adjusted or changed to make it work. The status quo advocates must put this failure behind them and move on to a new strategy. This time the United States should start with a market-based drug control strategy, and install only the controls necessary to bring drug use down to a manageable level. At the same time, design a public health system that provides honest information and education to discourage new drug users from picking up the habit.

8

MOTHER OF ALL BATTLES
The final battle to end the War on Drugs

Every war has its defining moment. The battle for the city of Stalingrad was the turning point in Hitler's fortunes in World War II. Napoleon had his Waterloo. Saddam Hussein called the battle for Kuwait, during Operation Desert Storm, the "Mother of All Battles," then saw his armies destroyed in a three-day battle. The upcoming battle to repeal drug prohibition in the U.S.A. will be the "Mother of All Battles" to restore sense to our nation's drug control policy.

Americans on both sides of the drug prohibition issue share the same goal, to prevent drug abuse, and share the same abhorrence of the recreational use of addictive drugs. The personal and social consequences of recreational drug use are such that no responsible person would defend the practice. Yet, as we have seen, there are passionate debates as to the best way for government to deal with the political, health, and social effects of the use of addictive psychoactive drugs for other than medical purposes. A majority of Americans support the government's policy of prohibiting drugs that are subject to abuse. But a majority also believe that the government's strategy to enforce drug prohibition has been a failure. This presents an interesting dichotomy: the American public support a drug control program that they believe to be a failure. Is America doomed to repeat the tragedy of the Vietnam War with its War on Drugs, because it can't remember history? The reader will recall reporter Thomas Lippman's words from Chapter 4: "Even when he and Johnson's other aides knew that their Vietnam strategy had little chance of success, McNamara writes, they pressed ahead with it, ravaging the land and sending young Americans to their deaths year after year, because they had no other plan."

Is the U.S.A. so impotent that its people will live with failure because the people and their leaders are fearful of trying another strategy? The United States did not have that kind of a society when your author was a boy and FDR told us, "All we have to fear is fear itself." Nor was it that kind of a society when Americans vanquished vicious enemies around

117

the globe in World War II, or when they answered the Soviet's blockade of Berlin with the airlift. Americans began to doubt themselves after the Vietnam War, but it looked as though America had regained its old "can-do" spirit with the Desert Storm victory. Now the United States is faced with the realization that its drug policy is in shambles and has utterly failed. Does today's American society have the fortitude to subdue its fear and deal with the drug problem forthrightly?

As Americans listen to the heated debate on drug prohibition they find that both sides have the same aims: (1) consistently reduce and prevent drug use; (2) eliminate the crime, corruption, and violence resulting from drug trafficking; and (3) reverse the massive cost of our present drug control policy. The present drug policy of the United States has accomplished none of these goals, and is never likely to do so. There is mounting empirical evidence that repealing drug prohibition will accomplish all of these objectives. This mountain of evidence in favor of a legal drug market makes it difficult to understand the phobia toward legal narcotics and cocaine exhibited by most Americans. But we begin to understand their fear when we recognize that there is one fundamental question that frames their objection to repealing drug prohibition. As commentators Evans and Novak would say, this is the *Big* question: "Will the repeal of drug prohibition result in increased drug use?"

Let the record speak for itself

To bring the record of drug prohibition fresh to our minds, let us review some of the salient points in U.S. drug history from Chapters 2 and 3. Tariff records of this country from 1840 to 1915, showed opium imports continually increasing until 1896, leveling off, and then decreasing.[1] The public's desire to further reduce the use of cocaine and the opiates in American society led to the passage of the Pure Food and Drug Act of 1906. This legislation did not restrict the sale, use, or advertising, of these drugs. It only required the listing of contents on food and drug labels; yet the effect of this information was enlightening. The act was responsible for an approximate one-third decline in sales of patent medicines containing narcotics in the four-year period following its passage. This decline in sales of opiate medications occurred while the sales of all patent medicines were increasing by 60% between 1902 and 1911.[2] Citizens of that day were expected to demonstrate

118

accountability for personal behavior even though narcotics and cocaine could be bought over-the-counter without restriction. Education of the public and government appeals for personal responsibility worked. The United States saw a further decline in the percentage of addicts in the population. An informed public responded when given the facts, and most Americans thereafter made a conscious effort to avoid addictive drugs.

Dr. Hamilton Wright's 1910 Report to Congress estimated opium addicts in the general population to be eighteen-hundredths of one percent, or 175,000 addicts in the 1909 population of approximately ninety million.[3] This compares favorably with the American Pharmaceutical Association committee's 1902 estimate of 200,000 addicts in a smaller population.[4] "[Professor David T.] Courtwright says Wright also set an unfortunate precedent, one familiar in subsequent efforts to address drug problems: He exaggerated addiction figures. The overall number of opiate addicts was declining, as were the importation and per capita consumption of opiates. But Wright sought to demonstrate that drugs were a large threat. So he massaged his figures to indicate that the problem was actually increasing."[5] After all, as the U.S. Opium Commissioner, he was trying to persuade a reluctant Congress of the need to pass restrictive drug legislation.

If today's population had the same ratio (0.18%) of narcotic addicts that Dr. Wright found in the 1910 population, the United States would now have 450,000 opiate addicts. Falco quotes figures from the office of the National Drug Control Policy for 1990, of 600,000 heroin addicts, as well as an additional 1.8 million hard-core cocaine addicts.[6] Estimates for 1993 show about 500,000 heroin addicts and 2.1 million hard-core cocaine users. Note that these estimates are by President Clinton's drug policy director, whose purpose is to celebrate declines from his office's 1988 estimates of 590,000 and 2.5 million. Even if these figures are accurate, the author would argue that they are hardly dramatic. Moreover, the report itself concedes that, because of the secrecy of drug trafficking the estimates are imprecise.[7] Empirical evidence demonstrates that unlimited access in a legal drug market does not automatically lead to increased drug use! It also demonstrates that prohibition with vigorous law enforcement does not lead to decreased drug use!

The federal government's change in strategy to accommodate the U.S. State Department's international opium protocol—first to institute drug controls with the Harrison Act, and then to completely ban these drugs on the basis of a U.S. Supreme Court ruling—started the United States on the rocky road of prohibition. It has been an expensive mistake in both lives and money, but even more of a tragedy because of the fear and violence it has brought to American communities. The United States is now a less pleasant place to live since the advent of drug dealers, the cocaine-cowboys, the posses, and the juvenile drug gangs. The criminalization of drug use has overwhelmed our courts. Long mandatory sentences, out of proportion to the crime committed, have caused jails to overflow. All these problems have been caused, and the U.S.A. still has every social and personal trauma from drug use that prohibition was supposed to eliminate.

Bureaucracy in Action

Chapter 4 covered the government's decision in 1914 to replace the laissez faire drug enterprise (a market mechanism) by imposing drug controls and eventually prohibition (a political mechanism). The Internal Revenue Service was originally designated to enforce drug prohibition. Over the years there have been many changes in the drug enforcement bureaucracy, but the one constant has been its ever expanding size and budget. The Narcotic Division began with 170 agents and a budget of $515,000 in 1920, but by 1995 the DEA personnel numbered 6,737, of which 3,433 were agents, with a budget of $756.5 million.[8] And this is only a fraction of the federal drug war budget of over $14 billion annually. In addition, the drug war also receives significant support from the Departments of Defense, Justice, and Treasury. Such a large bloated bureaucracy has the power base, political influence, and resources to perpetuate itself.

When people's careers are threatened they will put up a "no-holds-barred" defense of their employment. We have all witnessed labor protests and demonstrations when corporate management tries to close a plant or relocate a factory. And we know the angry passion of bureaucrats when Congress tries to close or cut back an agency. Your author experienced the bureaucratic "buzz saw" when once he suggested transferring operating control of a project from a civilian in headquarters to a military officer on-site. Thus hell hath no fury like that of the federal drug enforcement agents when someone suggests the legalization of drugs.

The difficulty of the fight ahead with the drug enforcement bureaucracy over efforts to effect meaningful change in this nation's drug control policy was evident when the Drug Enforcement Administration held an Anti-Legalization Forum at the FBI/DEA training Academy in August 1994. The purpose and product of this forum was a DEA guide entitled *"How To Hold Your Own in a Drug Legalization Debate."* This high-level DEA forum included drug war representatives from institutions, organizations, and major city police forces from across the nation. It is a sad commentary indeed that this was not a forum to improve the effectiveness of the War on Drugs, but was for the single purpose of combating the arguments of persons calling for change in the nation's anti-drug strategy. This was a forum to retain the entrenched bureaucracy and to protect the careers of the drug warriors. Professor Milton Friedman expounded upon this obstacle in a speech to the Drug Policy Foundation:

> [The drug bureaucracy] can command the attention of the media to make reform or repeal seem not respectable, not reasonable. After all, they will say over and over, the people who urge the legalization of drugs are simply ignorant or naive or don't understand what's going on. We, they will say, are the experts and know what works and what doesn't.
>
> How do we make the vested interests of government change their policy?...One way that has been effective in eliminating or reducing bad government programs is private competition. ...Unfortunately, however, private competition is not an effective solution as long as the government completely prohibits some drugs. ...In such areas, we do need to change the law.
>
> My thesis can be expressed in two main points. First, do not fool yourself into thinking that solutions will in fact work that simply involve changing the way the political mechanism is used. They will not escape the defects common to the political mechanism wherever it is used.... The second lesson I believe that we should learn, and it's probably the more important lesson, is that we are likely to make more progress against the war on drugs if we recognize that repealing drug prohibition is part of the broader problem of cutting down the scope and power of the government and restoring power to the people.[9]

Public hysteria works against reason.

There is as much hysteria connected to addictive drugs now as there was during World War I. During that war, New York State enacted the Whitney Act to provide proper and humane treatment and cure for the addict. (At that time, narcotics and cocaine were still legal with a physician's prescription.) Some expressed fear that as many as 500,000 addicts would return from the war. A Preliminary Report of the [New York] Secretary of the Treasury was quoted as evidence that thousands of draftees were being rejected in New York because of preexisting addiction, and that perhaps 200,000 addicts between ages 21 and 31 lived in New York. Actually, of 2,510,791 men examined nationwide at local draft boards, 1488 addicts were discovered, of whom 54 were permitted to enter the service. Only 383 came from New York State.[10]

Further evidence of gross inflation of the addict problem came in 1920 from the New York State Department of Narcotic Drug Control. "After the department had been functioning for a year, [Commissioner Walter C.] Herrick estimated that there were about 39,000 addicts in the state, of whom 13,000 were registered through the physician by whom they were treated. This total is substantially less than such figures as 200,000 which the Whitney Committee [in 1918] had accepted as reasonable."[11] Several states, including New York, were operating drug clinics with reasonable success, but pressure from the federal authorities closed all state drug clinics in the 1920s.

Dr. David Musto, in his book on the history of narcotics control, points out that "Peaks of overestimation have come before or at the time of the most repressive measures against narcotic use, as in 1919 when a million or more addicts and five million Parlor Reds were said to threaten the United States. Both groups were the object of severe penalties, although in retrospect both figures appear to have been enormously inflated."[12]

From where does this fear come? The people who originally proposed prohibition as a solution created this fear of drug addicts beyond anything that facts would support. They exaggerated the number of addicts in this country, overstated the impact of drug use by ethnic and racial minorities in our society, and ignored the reductions in drug use that occurred from public education about its dangers. They also failed to foresee the disastrous consequences of crime in the nation resulting from drug and alcohol prohibition.

There were strong racial overtones to the enactment of controls on the opiates, cocaine, and marijuana, with some of the reformers pointing to the minorities as being the primary abusers—tying cocaine abuse to the Negro, opium smoking to the Chinese, and marijuana use to the Mexicans. These scare tactics were used to justify the repressive solution the reformers proposed to employ—prohibition by force of law.[13] But there was one thing that the prohibitionists never considered—the fact that they might be wrong and that prohibition would make matters worse.

In a more recent example of drug hysteria, Mathea Falco cites the Lee Robins study that claimed one in five (20%) of the Vietnam veterans was returning to this country addicted to heroin.[14] "...Only 2 percent of the veterans continued to use heroin a year after returning to the United States. This dramatic reduction suggests that changed circumstances can have a profound effect on drug use, even among those addicted. In contrast to Vietnam, where heroin was cheap, easily available, and widely tolerated—as it would be here if it were legal—heroin in the United States was expensive, difficult to obtain, and subject to strong social disapproval."[15] This is a very conflicting statement. Any addict will tell you it is not difficult to obtain heroin anywhere in the U.S., and disapproval of drug use in the military is as strong, or stronger, than it is in civil life. So we must conclude that either: only a few soldiers were truly addicted; or heroin is not as addictive as we had been led to believe; or that the United States has found a cure for heroin addiction that is 98% effective.

While your author disagrees with her assessment of addicted Vietnam veterans, Mathea Falco is an important voice in the drug policy debate in this country. She obviously has the attention of the Clinton Administration with her book *The Making of a Drug Free America— Programs That Work,* in which she recommends a major shift in priorities to reducing the demand for drugs, rather than concentrating on supply reduction. She opposes legalizing narcotics and cocaine, but would obviously like some form of decriminalization for drug use so that drug abusers could be treated in the same environment as abusers of alcohol or tobacco.[16] She defends her prohibition stand in one way by stating that if drugs were legal in the United States, heroin would be cheap, easily available, and widely tolerated, as she believes it was in

Vietnam.[17] Yet she acknowledges that addictive drug use was generally despised, not tolerated, by the American public during the period of legal drugs in the early 20th century. She also acknowledges that there was less drug abuse when America had legal drugs than under drug prohibition today, and suggests, but fails to acknowledge, that drug abuse was declining in America's legal drug market before prohibition.[18] Mathea Falco's recommended emphasis on demand reduction has the enthusiastic support of your author, but it does not go far enough in that it does nothing to eliminate the greater problem of illegal drug trafficking.

There are more then enough drugs on our streets to meet all the needs of those desiring drugs. Heroin on the street has become cheaper and more pure. Six persons died from inadvertent overdose of almost pure heroin in the Lowell, Massachusetts area during one week in June 1995. Not only is there an adequate supply of cocaine and heroin, there also are underground laboratories manufacturing all kinds of new designer drugs. If you want it, you can get it! Demand drives the market. Available supply controls the price. Granted, lower price encourages greater use, but if price is relatively consistent, the consumption of legal drugs will be similar to the consumption of illegal drugs. An adjustment in taxes on legally supplied drugs can keep drugs available at a cost near today's street prices of illicit drugs, yet not so high as to encourage smuggling.

The status-quo advocates fail to understand that illegal drugs create a powerful motivation for criminal opportunists to lure the unwary into drug addiction for monetary gain. They have overlooked the barricades to their drug prevention efforts thrown up by the sales force of entrepreneurial drug peddlers, described in Chapter 5. Once again, harken to this book's warning that we cannot disregard the effectiveness of drug peddlers in pushing the use of drugs on our youth. Drug traffickers' pyramid sales forces are very effective and are in the best tradition of the American free enterprise system. To legalize drugs is to remove the impediment of drug pushers to our efforts to get people to refrain from drug use; to get off drugs if they are on them; and, once off drugs, to stay off drugs.

A dichotomy—legal drugs in a moral, vibrant society

On one hand, the United States before drug prohibition had legal narcotics and cocaine sold openly, like any other drugs. On the other hand, that society was reducing drug use and assuming a role of moral leadership in the world. The nation was thriving with a generally vibrant economy. It was hardly a cesspool of crime and moral degeneracy—which is the scenario most people fear will occur if this nation would return to legal narcotics and cocaine.

Professor James Q. Wilson is a highly respected scholar with a reputation for being able to assess facts to arrive at a reasonable conclusion. (Wilson is the Collins professor of management and public policy at U.C.L.A.) In 1972, President Nixon appointed him chairman of the National Advisory Council for Drug Abuse Prevention. The council, created by Congress, was charged with providing guidance on how best to coordinate the national War on Drugs. Writing in 1990, Wilson reported:

> I do not recall that we even discussed legalizing heroin, though we did discuss (but did not take action on) legalizing a drug, cocaine, that many people then argued was benign. Our marching orders were to figure out how to win the war on heroin, not to run up the flag of surrender.
>
> That same year, the eminent economist Milton Friedman published an essay in Newsweek in which he called for legalizing heroin. His argument was on two grounds: as a matter of ethics, the government has no right to tell people not to use heroin (or to drink or to commit suicide); as a matter of economics, the prohibition of drug use imposes costs on society that far exceed the benefits.
>
> That was 1972. Today, we have the same number of heroin addicts that we had then—half a million, give or take a few thousand. Having that many heroin addicts is no trivial matter; these people deserve our attention. But not having had an increase in that number for over fifteen years is also something that deserves our attention. What happened to the 'heroin epidemic' that many people once thought would overwhelm us?[19]

Wilson sets up a "straw man" with the prediction of a heroin epidemic, then knocks it for a loop by bragging that the epidemic never occurred. More importantly, the 1990 government estimate for heroin addicts in the United States was 600,000. That is an increase of 100,000 heroin addicts in an eighteen-year period when the federal government conducted an all-out War on Drugs and increased the drug-fighting budget from a few hundred million dollars to over $13 billion annually. What kind of success is that? Even "not having an increase," if true, could hardly be called a victory. Moreover, Professor Wilson would probably consider it rude for the author to mention the huge increase in cocaine use during this same period, or to recount the increase in crimes and killings related to drug trafficking. Could a legitimate drug market be worse? It wasn't before the U.S.A. passed prohibition.

Listening to Professor Wilson chortle about preventing a heroin epidemic reminds me of the old vaudeville routine with a strange little man walking down New York's 5th Avenue and ever so often sprinkling some powder from a can. A bystander observed him sprinkling the powder as he walked by and was prompted to ask, "Why are you sprinkling that powder on the sidewalk?"

"It keeps the elephants away," he replied, without missing a step.

"Keeps the elephants away? There are no elephants on 5th Avenue," exclaimed the bystander.

"You see, it works," said the little man as he continued on his way.

In reply to one of his critics, Wilson writes: "Ansley Hamid blames drug abuse on the fact that drugs are illegal. If they weren't, there would be less abuse. How does he know this. Because we had less before 1914. I only wish he had bothered to list all the ways the world has changed since 1914."[20] The fact that drug use was decreasing in the legitimate drug market before prohibition has been emphasized many times throughout this book. It is the most significant factor to consider while the United States ponders returning to a legal drug market. It does not matter how the world has changed since 1914. Even if those changes affect drug use in America, they have no bearing on this central fact: In preprohibition America, the legal and freely available drug supply did not prevent a decrease in the use of addicting psychoactive drugs. This same phenomenon is observable in the decrease in drinking and smoking occurring in our society today in spite of an unlimited and legal supply of alcohol and tobacco. Demand determines supply, and demand for these products is determined by societal attitudes toward the underlying vices.

Wilson glosses over the fact that the rate of drug addictions has increased 300% since 1914, by saying it's a different world today. But the more things change, the more they remain the same. Consider this. While the drug warriors patted themselves on the back for stopping a heroin epidemic after 1972, our State Department briefed Congress on April 4, 1994, to brace themselves for a heroin epidemic: "In the past five years, there has been a steady increase in the flow and purity of heroin to the U.S., suggesting that the taste for the drug is growing." [21] Does that sound familiar? The report alleged that drug corruption had infected officials and institutions in a long list of countries, including Bolivia, Burma, Kenya, Lebanon, Nigeria, Panama, Syria, Thailand, Venezuela, and Zambia. Assistant Secretary of State Robert Gelbard has said that 35 to 40 percent of all heroin arriving in the United States is brought by Nigerians.

Alcohol prohibition changed the American society considerably in the 13 years the citizens tolerated it. But Americans had the good sense to repeal it and the moral climate improved greatly from the Roaring Twenties to the Depression Thirties. With repeal, the U.S.citizenry also eliminated a lot of racketeering mobs, bootleggers, operators of speakeasies, and corrupt officials on-the-take. Now that group has been resurrected as drug cartels, drug dealers, operators of crack-houses, and corrupt officials on-the-take. (Corrupt officials will be with us always.) There is a lot of evidence that legalization would lead to less drug abuse and no evidence that continuing the drug ban for another 75 years would help the drug problem. James Q. Wilson takes pride in the fact that his council ignored Friedman's admonition to legalize drugs, thereby allegedly preventing a heroin epidemic. One of the best minds of our generation, Professor Friedman always speaks with great wisdom and logic, but unfortunately his ideas are generally a generation ahead of the majority. Professional pride will probably prevent Wilson from ever supporting the legalization of drugs, but before the end of this century, common sense will prevail. The majority of Americans will see the wisdom of Friedman's position and will demand an end to this eternal and fruitless war.

The Enemy Is Us

It's prohibition, stupid

Readers are all well aware of the sign that hung over campaign manager James Carville's desk during President Clinton's successful campaign for the presidency: "It's the economy, stupid." He forcefully and effectively kept the focus of the campaign on that essential theme by frequently tweaking campaign workers with that statement. In like manner, politicians should focus their effort on the single item that will allow us to successfully end our War on Drugs. The federal, state and municipal governments do not have to spend more money, or increase their effort, in the fight to reduce drug use. A change in strategy centering on the repeal of drug prohibition will do the job nicely. Regarding drug policy, the slogan should be: It's prohibition, stupid!

Some economists have estimated that the underground economy costs the United States government fully one-fourth of potential revenues. A large chunk of the underground economy is the illegal drug economy, estimated conservatively as being over one hundred billion dollars a year. It's a cash economy that pays no taxes, produces no benefit to the community, yet sucks the life-blood from the municipal social-support systems, while corrupting the very governmental organizations set against it.

Our experiences with tobacco

Let us look at our experiences with tobacco. Nicotine has never been banned or prohibited, even though over four hundred thousand Americans die prematurely each year and hundreds of thousand more suffer with debilitating health problems from the effects of tobacco use. Then there is the harm that tobacco brings on our society from the fires caused by the careless handling of smoking materials, or the discomfort and health hazards suffered by nonsmokers who have to breathe noxious fumes. The latest research indicates that there is a deleterious health consequence to second-hand smoke to those around smokers, especially children in a house or car with smoking parents.

With approximately fifty million nicotine addicts still remaining in the U.S.A., does anyone believe we should take away their tobacco and save them from their own destructive habit? A handful of people suggest banning tobacco as a solution. If prohibition worked, the answer would be yes, but it doesn't work. Ban tobacco and the government will spend more than it is spending on the drug war to try to control contraband cigarettes. There is no need to consider such a draconian move, because we have a solution that is in place and working. We are persistently and consistently reducing tobacco use in this country without a ban.

During World War II approximately sixty-seven percent of the adult male population in the United States smoked. Now approximately twenty-five percent of adult males smoke. Women's statistics are also encouraging, but teenager's statistics are not. The U.S. campaign to reduce the use of tobacco started with Surgeon General Luther Terry's report of 1964 on Smoking and Health. Dr. Terry's initiative has been sustained and reinforced by successive Surgeon Generals, appointed by Presidents from both political parties. Former Surgeon General Edwin Koop labeled nicotine as our most addictive drug. Antonia Novello, the Surgeon General appointed by President Bush, attacked the tobacco companies for using advertising with cartoon characters such as "Joe Camel" that, according to surveys by the Journal of the American Medical Association, were seducing minors to smoke. By any standard, the anti-smoking program has been remarkably successful in reducing the use of tobacco in the U.S.A. This success is in spite of the fact that nicotine is a highly addictive drug and that smoking has had a long history of acceptance in this country. How then has the government been so successful in reducing this drug's use and so totally unsuccessful in reducing the use of some other addicting drugs, especially the opiates and cocaine?

First, the government did its research and had conclusive proof that smoking was the primary culprit in causing early death from cancer, heart disease, and respiratory disease. The facts were laid before the public without scare tactics or hysteria. The medical profession was urged to bring these facts to the attention of their patients and point out to nicotine addicts that to quit smoking was the quickest and most positive way to improve their health. The tobacco companies counter-attacked vigorously and did everything they could to discredit the Surgeon General's facts. But, in the minds of the public, the government health officials won that battle.

To the credit of members of Congress, they banned cigarette advertising from television and radio shortly after the Surgeon General issued his report. Unfortunately, tobacco companies were still allowed to promote their products and advertise in the print media and on outdoor billboards. In spite of government restrictions to thwart their efforts, the tobacco hucksters have found many subtle and ingenious methods to seduce potential new addicts.

Second, the government started a campaign of education to encourage those who smoked to quit, and those who had not started smoking, to refrain. There have been counter-advertising campaigns through public service commercials to demonstrate the folly of continuing this dangerous habit and showing the benefits to a person who can throw off this addiction. Surprisingly, there was no immediate or massive response to the Surgeon General's damning information, but slowly and steadily the message is being heeded. Tobacco companies are also required to place warning labels on their products to advise users of their potential harm. Many skeptics have downplayed the effectiveness of the warning labels, and as far as their being immediately effective, the skeptics are probably right, but there is a long term residual effect in reinforcing the message that the health authorities are trying to convey.

Third, the government—all levels from national to municipal—has gradually and effectively added regulations to protect nonsmokers from the toxic fumes of smokers by specifying where and when they can smoke. Even the most avid anti-smoking crusader could never in his wildest imagination have envisioned, in 1964, that within 30 years smoking in the United States would be banned in aircraft, public conveyances, public buildings, hospitals, and work places.

Fourth, the general population has almost made a pariah of the smoker with the same general disgust that ended the spittoon and tobacco chewing in public places some fifty years ago. There is no more ardent advocate for clean air in public places than a reformed smoker. Smokers are motivated to give up the habit by the desire to be socially acceptable. The new message is, "You may have come a long way, baby, but it is time to give up that obnoxious habit."

Crop "supports" were started in the 1930s as a "New Deal" device to help farmers hurt by the Great Depression. Tobacco was included among supported crops since the U.S. government did not start campaigning against its use until 1964. Your author has always opposed government subsidies as an inefficient form of help to any group including farmers. Now that smoking is so widely disapproved, few Americans believe that tobacco farmers should be subsidized to grow a product so obviously harmful to the life and health of our society. Subsidizing tobacco when the government is trying to discourage its use, and subsidizing coca farmers in the Andes country to grow an alternative crop, are two candidate programs for early elimination as senseless expenditure of funds.

While much progress has been made in the smoking-reduction program, there is still much that could be done to create a more positive anti-smoking climate. Smoking among American adults continued to decline in the mid-1990s, according to a survey by the U.S. Centers for Disease Control and Prevention. In 1993, the percentage of all adults who smoke was 25, down from 26.3 the year before. For women the figures were even better, 22.5% in 1993 as against 24.8% in 1992. Also encouraging was the finding that 70% of smokers said they wanted to quit. The most discouraging finding was that smoking among teenagers had jumped up from 17% to 19%. Such a trend, if continued, could wipe out progress among adults. The tobacco companies spent almost two billion dollars in advertising and promotion to make this happen. Tobacco companies still promote and encourage smoking through many devious devices. Gratuitous smoking by performers in movies and television frequently has the imprint of "payola." Former Surgeon General Novello summarized the threat: "Cigarettes are the most heavily advertised and promoted products in the United States. In constant dollars, expenditures for cigarette advertising and promotion have increased threefold since 1975. Recently, as seen with my friend 'the Camel,' this advertising has been increasingly aimed at our young people. A recent study in the Journal of the American Medical Association showed that this campaign, which the industry claims is not aimed at children, has been far more successful in marketing cigarettes to children than was expected. The end result of this campaign is that the illegal sale of Camels to minors has skyrocketed from $6 million to $476 million." [22]

The Enemy Is Us

Ban all advertising and promotion of tobacco

Prohibition of tobacco would be as counterproductive as prohibition of alcohol and drugs, so banning tobacco is not a viable option. At the very least let the tobacco industry pay its own way without subsidies, and let free enterprise reign. But we have seen that restricting advertising on television has had a positive effect on reducing smoking in America. Banning all tobacco advertising and promotion would be the most positive step that the United States could take in its anti-smoking campaign. Then combining the anti-smoking program with a strong counter-advertising campaign would give America a one-two punch to stop the smoking menace cold. Tobacco companies' sponsorship of sporting events in particular is galling, when we are trying to encourage our young people to participate in sports as a mean to a more healthful life. Tobacco companies were recently found to be in violation of the television advertising ban by strategically placing billboards in stadiums behind goalposts, adjacent to scoreboards, or other areas that television cameras would focus on in the natural course of televising a sporting event. This was a calculated ploy to promote their products. Do we need the Marlboro Man, Joe Cool, the camel, or their ilk, smirking from the fences of the ball park, or the arena, in an attempt to thwart the public health message?

We are seeing evidence every year that the U.S. campaign to improve the health of the nation by reducing the number of smokers is working. Education is a must. Punitive taxes alone will not work. Evidence abounds. For instance, a study was presented at a 1993 American Heart Association conference on heart disease prevention, by Stanton A. Glantz of the University of California, San Francisco. A summary of the study follows:

California voters passed a referendum in 1988 that increased cigarette taxes by 25 cents per pack and required that 20 percent of the tax money be used for smoking cessation programs. An early study showed that the $28 million, 18 months TV campaign increased the rate at which smokers quit smoking. Before the campaign, cigarette consumption was falling by 46 million packs per year in California. During the campaign, from April 1990 to September 1991, consumption fell at a rate of 164 million packs per year, triple what the decrease had been. When the

132

campaign was suspended, the decline in cigarette sales eased off to 19 million packs per year.

A new study looked at the effects on cigarette sales. In the three and one half years of the TV campaigns, the decline in cigarette sales cost the tobacco industry $1.1 billion. Some have suggested that the tax increase itself was responsible for the decline in cigarette consumption. Glantz addressed that issue by looking at smoking rates in Nevada, which adopted a 25 cent-per-pack tax increase at the same time California did. Without the ad campaign, however, Nevada's cigarette consumption rates were not significantly affected. Dr. Thomas E. Novotny of the Centers for Disease Control and Prevention said the study was a convincing demonstration of the campaign's effectiveness.[23]

Comparing nicotine to the other addicting drugs, such as heroin, morphine and cocaine, is not intended to convey the idea that a hard-core drug addict is no worse than a cigarette smoker. The intention is to compare methods of reducing cigarette smoking, which is as addictive as heroin or cocaine, to methods of reducing the use of hard-core drugs. The principles are the same in both cases. The U.S.A. is achieving success in reducing the number of nicotine addicts. It has failed miserably in reducing hard-core drug use. The difference? Cigarettes are legal; heroin and cocaine are not. It is more effective to educate and persuade, and to treat addiction in a legitimate climate than it is to criminalize substances and to enforce abstinence at the end of a gun barrel. We need to apply some of the lessons learned from the successful campaigns of public health agencies in reducing cigarette smoking.

U.S. experience with alcohol

Experience with alcohol paralleled that of narcotics and cocaine until 1933, when prohibition of alcohol ended with the repeal of the 18th amendment to the U.S. Constitution. Alcohol is the nation's most widely used drug and creates more addicts than any drug other than nicotine. We are lulled into complacency over alcohol use, since most people can use it in moderation throughout their lifetimes without a problem. Many people will, on occasion, drink to a point of intoxication, where their judgment and reflexes are impaired for a few hours, rendering them a danger to themselves and others. Then there are the approximately fourteen million Americans who are classified as alcohol addicts. While all alcoholics share the common identifying trait of dependency, they can range from the heavy-drinking working man who can still function reasonably effectively to the skid-row wino who cares about nothing else other than the next drink. The drunkard is as much a pitiful creature as the junky, enslaved by his addiction and lacking those qualities of humanity that give a person character and personality.

There were many good reasons to repeal alcohol prohibition, not the least of these was that it didn't accomplish the goal it was supposed to achieve. In repealing alcohol prohibition, the federal government essentially withdrew from regulating, controlling, or enforcing laws against the sale and manufacture of alcoholic drinks, leaving it to the states to establish their own levels of control. Three states retained prohibition of alcohol after the national repeal of the 18th Amendment. Of course, there always has been considerable variation from state to state in laws pertaining to alcohol.

Daniel K. Benjamin and Roger LeRoy Miller, in their book *Undoing Drugs—Beyond Legalization,* propose that the federal government withdraw all legislation prohibiting use of recreational drugs and leave the enforcement and regulation of these substances to the individual states, as was done with alcohol upon the repeal of the 18th Amendment. They refer to this plan as the "Constitutional Alternative," and believe that the decentralization of regulation and control will result in each state having drug controls more to its liking and circumstances. Some states will enact lenient legislation and some probably more stringent laws than present federal controls.

Benjamin and Miller believe that some states will find better solutions that will serve as examples for all. In short, fifty legislatures, rather than Congress, would try to solve the overall drug problem. All the subordinate problems that face the entire nation would still face each state. It would seem to this author appropriate for Congress to seek the counsel of the state governors as a basis for the general framework of a federal program to achieve some national uniformity. States that legalize drugs or enact easier regulations would experience an influx of addicts and drug tourists not unlike the experience of the Netherlands as the most lenient drug country in the European community. An important consideration is to insure that every individual has federal authority to legally possess personal amounts of drugs regardless of state law. Individual states could then regulate and restrict the program within federal constraints to suit their individual circumstances. In some areas of concern, federal control is needed to deal with foreign governments, or for problems that extend across state boundaries—such as the present restrictions on advertising liquor and tobacco on radio and television. It is probable that many of Benjamin's and Miller's ideas will be incorporated in any reform of our present drug laws.

American society has not been as effective in moderating its drinking habits to match its success in reducing tobacco use. Americans have reduced their consumption of hard spirits in favor of the lighter beers and wines, and have had some success in reducing alcohol-related traffic deaths in recent years. Public service advertising and outraged citizen organizations, such as MADD (Mothers Against Drunk Drivers), are creating public intolerance of drunks. Binge drinkers, even those who get drunk only once a year and drive, entail a risk of killing someone during those few hours of intoxication as great as if they were full-time alcoholics. The designated driver program has been most successful in helping to prevent such tragedies, but no one can shirk his or her own responsibility. Here is the author's rule: You were sober when you took the first drink, so the responsibility for whatever happens after that is yours.

Irresponsible alcohol advertising

Our efforts to discourage drinking are destroyed when we allow the beer and wine manufacturers to advertise and promote their products in a way that is especially appealing to young people. If you watch the television beer commercials, you see that a six-pack of beer miraculously causes beautiful bikini-clad girls to appear out of nowhere, ready to party and have a good time. Beer means party time! That's the message that comes across, and it is a great inducement for young people to indulge. Wine makers convey the image of celebration for their product. To drink is to celebrate the good times, and many of those seduced by alcohol advertisements do not have the maturity to appreciate the consequences of over-indulgence. It will be difficult to make headway toward a more sober America as long as we condone the seduction of our youth with the advertising and promotion of the breweries and the wineries. While they claim they are not targeting the young, the youths see the same ads we see. What young man wouldn't be tempted to buy a six-pack when he sees that ad where a guy pops the cap off a bottle of beer and a bevy of scantily clad beauties suddenly appear?

Recently there have appeared a number of advertisements by the alcoholic beverage manufacturers urging responsible drinking and cautioning parents to stop underage drinking before it gets started. The industry is commended for using this advertising avenue to remind America that substance abuse is everyone's concern. If the industry cannot also turn off the seductive commercials, the public may demand restrictions not to the distillers' liking. In his history of the Roaring Twenties, *Only Yesterday*, Frederick Lewis Allen points out one reason Americans voted for prohibition: "The wet leadership was discredited; for it was furnished by the dispensers of liquor, whose reputation had been unsavory and who had obstinately refused to clean house even in the face of a growing agitation for temperance."[24] Few Americans are proposing prohibition of alcohol again, but the alcohol industry might wisely consider refraining from advertising that entices or seduces youths, or glorifies drinking. Such content comprises the bulk of the beer and wine ads. If such restraint is not shown, the industry will see a growing movement to ban all advertising and promotion of alcohol. Should no producer of alcoholic beverages be allowed to advertise or promote his product, then all companies would be competing on a level field. A few years back, Coors beer became one of the most popular beers east of the Mississippi river before it was either distributed or advertised. Individuals would transport a case or a car-full back East and distribute it among their friends. The success of the original Hershey bar without advertising proved that a good product doesn't have to be advertised to be accepted and purchased by the public. The alcoholic beverage companies should think of the advertising money that could go directly to the profit line and stop glamorizing drinking for young people. It's called "being a good citizen."

One can be sure that most elements of the media will join with the alcohol producers to lobby Congress in opposition to eliminating beer, wine, and liquor advertising. The television media strongly opposed the loss of cigarette advertising revenues in 1965. The print media and outdoor advertisers were successful in retaining their media for the tobacco companies. Your author has little confidence in corporations' ability to refrain from promoting their products, even if harmful or subject to abuse, and believes that all advertising of tobacco, alcohol, and recreational drugs should be banned if this nation is really serious about improving the health and general welfare of the American society. Such a sacrifice seems a small price to pay to correct some of the worst ills of a beloved country. All citizens feel resentment when a government decision affects their business, but many manufacturers have adjusted operations for the common good—including the makers of asbestos, DDT, and silicone. Distillers of hard spirits voluntarily decided not to advertise their products on television.

Prescription drug junkies

A Miami investigative reporter recently described his experience in trying to buy Percodan by phone. Percodan is a potent painkiller and one of America's most abused and addictive legal drugs. He called 14 pharmacies using the name of a nonexistent doctor and ordered 12 Percodan tablets at each. Eleven turned him down, but three filled his order. The reporter, Derek Reveron, said that addicts come up with some pretty sophisticated schemes to beat legal safeguards. They usually write prescriptions, using forms and DEA identification numbers stolen from real doctors. If the druggist checks a prescription the junky often has an accomplice to "verify" the order at an ordinary telephone booth.[25]

Somehow many Americans have the idea that addiction to legally prescribed drugs is to be pitied and not condemned. In a too frequent type of case, a physician was negligent in monitoring his patient, but in a typical case the patient knew he was becoming excessively dependent and resorted to devious methods to obtain additional prescriptions for the drug. Such a prescription pill junky is just as much an addict as a habitual user of crack cocaine. Somehow the prescription-drug addict usually is recommended for treatment in a rehabilitation institution and receives the sympathy of friends and family. The crack-cocaine addict most frequently receives scorn and jail. Whether sources are legal or illegal, it is difficult to keep drugs from a determined addict without putting in such stringent safeguards that a community ties up the normal course of commerce. Legalization of the recreational drugs would also tend to eliminate the illegal traffic in prescription drugs.

Chapter summary:

The points made in this chapter can be set forth as a set of maxims:

• "In problem solving the key is what strategy we use to solve them," according to management expert Stephen Covey.

• "Do not fool yourself into thinking that solutions will in fact work that simply involve changing the way the political mechanism [prohibition] is used."—Milton Friedman

• "Repealing drug prohibition is part of the broader problem of cutting down the scope and power of the government and restoring power to the people."—Milton Friedman

• Drug use decreased in America's legal drug market during the two decades before prohibition.

• An educated and informed American public will make the right personal decisions.

• Hysteria and fear of drugs should not prevent a reform of the U.S. drug policy.

• Americans are paying a terrible price for the War on Drugs.

• Legalization will have far less social costs than prohibition.

• It will pay the United States monetarily to repeal drug prohibition.

• Our experiences with tobacco and alcohol serve as models for a drug-control policy.

9

RETREAT, HELL—
We Will Attack From A Different Direction

This soldier is not retiring from the battle and surrendering the field to the substance abusers. Rather, your author offers a change of strategy in the War on Drugs that focuses the attack directly upon the object of our society's problem—the recreational drug abuser. This attack will accomplish the nation's objective to reduce recreational drug use to manageable levels. As stated earlier, once the United States returns all drug commerce to a legitimate enterprise, the nation will have eliminated the worst results of the War on Drugs: the power of drug cartels, dealers, pushers, and gangs, as well as the corruption of our officials and institutions. The anti-drug bureaucracies at all levels of government can be demobilized. Drug prevention, education, and treatment of the individual can receive the nation's full attention when society no longer has to contend with the criminal aspect of the drug problem.

Public health officials have given us convincing evidence that habitual uses of alcohol, heroin, cocaine, marijuana, or tobacco are all harmful to the individual and to society. It is improbable that society will ever persuade all citizens to abstain from the use of these substances. So we must continue to educate the people and to devise prevention programs that discourage drug use. We must provide effective care and treatment, as well, that will minimize the harm resulting from drug abuse and addiction. Like nuclear technology, psychoactive substances are a part of our culture and cannot be banished, willed, or wished away. We must learn to deal with the situation without hysteria, or without skewering our economy and domestic tranquillity on the prongs of an ill-advised strategy that creates more problems than it solves.

First, let us address control of the currently illegal drugs—heroin, cocaine, and marijuana—because these drugs are the cause of most of the drug-trafficking crime. Later we will consider the legal drugs of nicotine and alcohol for inclusion in the drug-control policy. Many

The Enemy Is Us

Americans use illegal substances on a frequent and even on a habitual basis without any apparent difficulty for years at a time. Many are "chippers"—the weekenders, or party-time users of dope, who refrain from daily use. All too frequently, at some time during their experimentation, casual use leads to abuse. Abuse results in disruptions in the user's personal relationships and sometimes in the ability to remain self-supporting. These users are the ones who fall over the line so that drugs now control their lives. Preventing this condition and treating the addict should be the primary focus of the new United States drug-control policy.

It is not an easy task to change stupid behavior, especially when a person plunges ahead into risky and reckless conduct with an attitude of "be damned with the consequences." To get a short-term euphoric high, some people will continue taking drugs in spite of daily reports of drug tragedies and public health warnings that drug use can destroy a career, wreck relationships, and cheat an individual of any opportunity for a purposeful life. It is frustrating to see adults continue to experiment with substances knowing full well that the outcome could be disastrous. It is not surprising, however, that teenagers, in the full illusion of their earthly immortality, are tempted to try these "pleasures." This is the reason we must concentrate on building character and moral values in our youth to enable them to exercise sound judgment that withstands these temptations.

Some people argue that, used in moderation, psychoactive substances do no harm. Cigarettes, not drugs, were the big "hang-up" during my youth, and my father never missed an opportunity to point out the folly of tobacco use. "Son," he would say, "some people will tell you, smoking doesn't hurt you, but I'm telling you that it can't do you any good, so why go to the expense and trouble to pick up the habit." Frequently he would point to a billboard with an endorsement of a cigarette by an athlete whom he knew I admired, and would mention that the man was a great athlete in spite of his smoking, not because of it. He didn't say these things once, but dozens of times over my growing up years. It was a repetitive message that became imbedded in my mind, and peer pressure to smoke did not prevail against it. Further, Dad taught by example. He used the same message and example in regard to alcohol.

Although my father was a man of faith, he used a common-sense approach to harmful substances. His philosophy was: If it doesn't do you any good, why do it? This philosophy deserves wider use in drug-prevention programs. Parents should be encouraged, as well as private and social agencies, to try a common-sense approach to avoiding harmful behavior. When parents are unwilling or unable to show their offspring the practical value of "saying no," schools and churches and organizations should do so. Yet it must be acknowledged that practical arguments are not enough for some young people—or people of any age, for that matter. Religious, ethical, and aesthetic appeals often must be added or must be the heart of the matter. Thus Alcoholics Anonymous has succeeded with drinkers unresponsive to purely practical arguments. Organizations similar to Alcoholics Anonymous are working with smokers, gamblers, spouse-abusers—and drug abusers. Fortunately an increasing number of churches have programs aimed at habits, including drug abuse, that keeps man separated from his creator. A more explicit religious appeal is the surest, and sometimes the only way to strengthen humans to change their lives: that is, a quest for redemption of one's life. In the words of Ezra Taft Benson, "The world would shape human behavior, but Christ can change human nature."[1]

In sum, the author's new battle plan will include a wide range of educational, preventive, and treatment programs. This new battle plan will reduce the use of addictive substances within society and will create a climate of social intolerance toward those who persist in using such substances to their own detriment. A free person has a right to choose how he or she will treat his or her body, but the freedom to choose also places the responsibility on the individual to use sound judgment and make good choices. Responsible individuals will ensure that their behavior does no harm to others, or does not create a burden on the community. Government at any level should not arbitrarily intervene in a person's life unless the individual's actions are harmful to someone else, or harmful to the welfare of the community. Minors, as noted elsewhere, should be subject to parental or governmental controls until they gain enough maturity to make responsible choices.

"A drug free America" is a catchy slogan and even a desirable goal, but like a "sinless society," it is not achievable in the world in which we must live. Most Americans strive for perfection in their individual lives and in their society, knowing that perfection is not obtainable but they should strive for it. America's goal is to reduce the use of harmful substances to the lowest possible level, and to minimize the harmful social side effects that accompany substance abuse. Yet we have unnecessarily burdened ourselves with a punitive criminal justice system to enforce a policy of prohibition that has not achieved a reduction in drug use, and besides is fraught with corruption and violence. The United States has a better strategy available that will cost the taxpayers nothing, save countless billions of dollars, and will provide tax revenues to pay for the most effective prevention and treatment programs available.

Would legalization mean a return to the unrestricted manufacture, sale, and use of drugs that existed before the enactment of the Harrison Act on December, 17, 1914? No, but the new plan builds on the pre-1914 situation. The reader will recall that the Harrison Act banned cocaine but permitted small amounts of narcotics in the numerous patent medicines sold over-the-counter. However, both narcotics and cocaine could be legally dispensed with a physician's prescription.[2] This provision resulted in a number of "dope doctors" writing prescriptions for a fee so that drug addicts could maintain their habits. Britain also had a similar experience with "dope doctors" when physicians in that country were authorized to write drug prescriptions for addicts. Reformers were disillusioned when they found that the requirement for prescriptions did not result in more responsible drug use than consumer's choice.

In hindsight, we see that restricting free access to recreational drugs by requiring a prescription is the point where black market activities begin. When Congress drafted the Harrison Act, it would have better served the people had it initiated a stronger drug education and prevention campaign, restricted the advertising and promotion of psychoactive substances, and restricted sales through pharmacists only. The limits on narcotics and cocaine in patent medicines as originally written in the Act appear to have been helpful, but the requirement of a prescription for these drugs was a step too far.

The Battle Plan

When asked what drug plan he favored, Milton Friedman, Nobel Laureate in economics, replied, "There is no chance whatsoever in the near future or the distant future of getting what I would really like, which is a free market. As a first step on the right road, I believe the right thing to do is to treat drugs, currently illegal drugs, exactly the same way you treat alcohol and tobacco. Not because that's the best way, not because that's the ideal arrangement, but because it's an arrangement that people know, that is in existence. It involves, in a certain sense, the least kind of change, so [the alcohol and tobacco models] seems to me the right direction in which to go—right direction in the sense again of a practical compromise, not of ultimate principle."[3]

This is the course that your author proposes. Before the 1914 Harrison Act the United States had the laissez-faire drug market that Professor Friedman desires. This free market was definitely less harmful and produced a lower ratio of addicts than today's black market in illegal drugs. However, our concern now is not to have the best economic model, nor to turn back the clock, but to reduce substance abuse within our society. We have seen some good results from America's anti-smoking and anti-drinking campaigns. We could incorporate into an anti-drug program similar regulatory features that would further discourage drug use in a legal drug market. Leave the free market mechanisms in the private sector to determine production, trade, and consumption of drugs, but utilize government-supported programs to discourage drug use and build societal intolerance of the drug habit. Using this model, drug use can be reduced further by:

(1) Restricting where, when, and how drugs can be used.

(2) Eliminating all favorable advertising and promotion.

(3) Using educational advertising to discourage recreational use.

(4) Prescribing standard generic formulas and packages for each drug type that can be marketed.

But one central principle must stand—all drugs need to be freely available to adults, and restrictions on their use should be the minimum needed for adequate control.

There are many ways to fight a war, or to fight drug abuse. Yet the best plan in either case is one that can accomplish the objective with the least expense, with the least loss of life, and with the least disruption of normal order. In constructing a new national drug policy, Congress should consider the American free enterprise model. The private sector has always served this nation well, and the United States should stay with the system that best supports liberty, freedom, and individual rights. Overarching this objective is the consideration that individual behavior should do no harm to others, and that Congress should achieve its policy with the least possible use of government control or regulation. This battle plan fits that description. There are cautions, however, in implementing this plan that the author will discuss later.

The Enemy Is Us

Half way measures won't do

Many opponents of drug prohibition feel that the government's position is so firmly planted in prohibition that to obtain any moderation of drug controls it will be necessary to work within the prohibition mechanism. Harm reduction is one such proposal. "Proponents of harm reduction policies typically favor an assortment of drug treatment programs including the use of methadone and other maintenance programs. They insist on the need for needle exchange programs. They recommend public health and community outreach efforts to maintain contact between health service providers and illicit drug users."[4] But even if harm reduction policies could be incorporated into the present drug control system we would still have most of the frustrations and problems that accompany prohibition.

A piecemeal approach to legalization, as has sometimes been suggested, would be dragging out the agony of the War on Drugs. Decriminalization is to remove criminal penalties for possession and use of illegal drugs while production and trade in the same drugs remain illegal, and subject to prosecution. It is disappointing to hear astute supporters of drug policy reform advocating such an approach, starting with decriminalization of marijuana and moving next to a weak cocaine product, and so on.[5] Remember, you cannot tinker with, or fine tune, a failed authoritarian political system to make it work—it must be overturned. It is the system that is wrong, not the application of the system. The prohibition enforcement bureaucracy is a political mechanism that has worked to the detriment of American society. Socialism in the Soviet Union was also an authoritarian political system that failed. It fell apart when Gorbachev tried to tinker with this authoritarian state by opening the society to provide more freedom to the Soviet people. It took just a little bit of liberty to overturn the Union of Soviet Socialist Republics.

Experience tells us to cut off the prohibition of drugs cleanly and completely. The author has confidence that this plan will work, because the United States has the historical precedent of legal psychoactive drugs from the beginning of the nation to the year 1920. It was also convincingly demonstrated in the first two decades of this century that the United States could reduce drug use and addiction rates in a legal drug market. To be sure there was a level of drug abuse before 1920. But it was during the hysteria of World War I and its aftermath when government officials over-reacted by initiating the prohibition of narcotics and cocaine. The U.S.A. also had the bad experience of alcohol prohibition from 1920 to 1933, which all but the most hidebound prohibitionist concedes was a failure. Finally, Americans have a more recent good experience with tobacco. The National Campaign to Reduce Smoking has led to a steady reduction in the use of this most addictive substance.

Anything that a reformer of the current drug policy hopes to accomplish with a half-way program can be better achieved with the complete repeal of drug prohibition. The United States has had legal heroin, cocaine, and marijuana before, and this nation controlled these drugs more effectively than it could ever hope to under drug prohibition where it has no control. The repeal of alcohol prohibition was accomplished in a single bold action—so let us do it for drugs.

The new strategy

Let the reader assume at this point that Congress and the President have recognized the mistake of drug prohibition and have revoked all laws that prohibit the production, trade, or consumption of currently illegal psychoactive addictive drugs. The United States will henceforth control and restrict these drugs in a legal market. The political experts will design the new Federal Drug Control Policy, using all the available evidence from our past, our current experience in controlling legal but potentially harmful substances, and the best and latest technology from science, medicine, and government.

At this point we can consider the War on Drugs over, replaced by a time to heal the wounds of the nation. The War on Drugs will be redefined as the National Campaign to Reduce Drug Use and Addiction. The United States can then begin to withdraw America's drug warriors from the drug battle outside U.S. borders, on the high seas, and in the air. At home, the huge drug enforcement bureaucracy can be dismantled or redirected to other governmental needs. Congress and the states can design a policy compatible with the existing prescription-drug marketplace, because the infrastructure and regulations for controls are already in place.

Currently illegal drugs will become legal "controlled drugs," to distinguish them from prescription drugs, which are used solely for medical purposes, and controlled because they have great potential for abuse or addiction. It will be made clear to the public, manufacturers, retailers, and purchasers that the government is controlling, restricting, and regulating psychoactive products in ways to discourage, yet not prohibit, their use. Political leaders will make clear why drug prohibition was repealed. Recreational drugs were again made legal primarily to keep criminals out of the drug business, to give citizens a freedom of choice, to eliminate the hypocrisy in law enforcement, and to reduce one form of government interference in private lives.

Who will be allowed to produce what?

Let the reader continue to imagine a policy of legalization. Specifically, any licensed pharmaceutical corporation will be authorized to manufacture and distribute heroin, cocaine, marijuana, and other psychoactive drugs, in a generic form, as prescribed and certified by the U.S. Food and Drug Administration. The FDA should authorize drugs that consumers want. Their authority would be to certify manufacturers' products of uniform quality, strength, and purity of ingredients. To prevent brand promotion, there will be standard packaging, with no brand names, logos, or manufacturer's names appearing on the packages. Labels will carry appropriate warnings of hazards to life or health, and a disclaimer of the manufacturer's liability for its use. A more detailed description of the drugs' hazards and side effects will be provided the consumer at the pharmacist's station. No favorable advertising or promotion of any nature will be permitted.

Drug corporations will be free to make their own arrangements under normal trade regulations for purchase and delivery of raw drugs from overseas or domestic sources, but all processing to the end product will be done within the United States. No shipments of psychoactive substances will be permitted outside this country without the express approval of the U.S. government and the government of the receiving nation. Pricing of the product will be the prerogative of manufacturers, wholesalers, and retailers, as long as it is in keeping with fair trade practices. All drug companies, small or large, will have the same opportunity to compete within the market with the same generic product.

Retreat, Hell!

Pricing and service will be the only competitive advantages a manufacturer can achieve.

A new strategy for the War on Drugs, as it pertains to the manufacture and distribution of controlled-drugs, has been presented in the preceding five paragraphs. The author's suggested procedures are intended to prevent corporate greed from replacing the plundering for profit now practiced by the foreign drug cartels. It would also prevent the callous greed displayed by United States corporations, as they shamelessly push their legal but lethal products containing nicotine and alcohol onto a youthful and impressionable American consumer. Congress and a Presidential Administration might also consider eliminating this seductive advertising and promotion of alcohol and tobacco and open the way for a more effective National Health Program to overcome substance abuse and addiction.

Who will sell what to whom?

Benjamin and Miller suggested a Constitutional Alternative, where the federal government would repeal its drug laws and step out of the picture, leaving it to the states to determine drug policy. They admit that this process would result in 50 different sets of drug laws, possibly ranging from a laissez-faire drug market in lenient states to complete prohibition in authoritarian states. However, the variations among state laws would cause considerable problems in and of themselves. New York found this to be true when it restricted legally available cocaine in 1913, only to find growing numbers of illegal peddlers on the streets who obtained an unlimited legal supply of cocaine in New Jersey, where there were no restrictions.[6] States and the federal government should coordinate efforts to establish some uniformity—such as national standards for the manufacture of generic drugs, how they are to be packaged, if or how mail orders can be utilized, as well as federal laws banning advertising and promotion of drugs anywhere in the U.S.A.

The states currently determine the retail sales mechanisms for prescription drugs, alcohol, and tobacco, and in all probability retailing of new legal controlled drugs would also come under state control. It is highly recommended that psychoactive drugs be controlled, as any highly potent drug, by state-licensed pharmacies. These drugs would be sold over-the-counter, without a prescription, to any adult obviously of age or anyone who can show proof of being over 21 years of age. To ensure the best possible control, sales should be transacted only at the pharmacist's station. Registered pharmacists are responsible professionals, familiar with drugs, controls, and laws covering dangerous substances. Each state currently has regulatory agencies in position to effect a smooth and immediate startup after the legalization of these drugs. With the retail drug apparatus already in place, it would appear to be the height of folly to duplicate this distribution system with a separate and contrived, politically-controlled bureaucracy.

State-operated recreational drug outlets, similar to state-operated liquor package stores, would probably be a poor choice to control drug sales, since such organizations tend to become involved in politics and patronage. Many states are not doing well with their state liquor stores, and there is a move to sell them off and privatize them. However, that is a decision for each state. Keeping the federal, state, and municipal governments out of the retail sales business, but with some governmental oversight of the private-sector drug business is a better and more effective strategy. The above actions would bring us back to where we were in the first decade of this century after the enactment of the Pure Food and Drug Act of 1906, except that now we will have some modest controls and regulations on the dispensing of these products. Another difference from the first two decades of this century would be that sales to minors would be prohibited.

Secondary sales of controlled-drugs by individuals or commercial establishments, such as bars or night clubs, should be illegal. It should also be a criminal offense for anyone to give another person a psychoactive drug or hallucinogen without that person's knowledge or permission. Before prohibition, many saloons would sometimes put a pinch of cocaine into drinks to give them a little extra kick. After legalization, the individual should be the only person making the decision to use or buy drugs. No "gatekeeper," such as a doctor or pharmacist, should be required to confirm one's personal decision. Give the individual the factual information to make an intelligent decision, and if he or she is bull-headed enough to ignore sound advise they are also determined enough to circumvent the decision of a doctor or pharmacist.

Particular emphasis should be placed on advising all users of psychoactive substances that the Surgeon General strongly advises against using these substances and the probable consequences of their use. A drug user today has no one but another drug user or pusher to advise him, should he have any questions about using the drug he is considering. Criminal acts committed by a user should not be excused on the ground that he or she was under the influence of a substance, especially since it was willfully self-administered. Failure to assume one's personal or civic responsibilities due to substance abuse should result in involuntary confinement in a treatment center. Those responsibilities include caring for your family, paying child support, paying taxes and license fees, taking license tests, or reporting for jury duty. A second failure in civic responsibilities should result in involuntary conscription into a rehabilitation conservation camp. Further failures should result in indefinite confinement in a disciplinary work barracks until rehabilitation occurs.

Once the enabling legislation is in place for a legitimate drug market, the President can declare peace in the War on Drugs. The daily violence from the drug war that this nation has endured for the past decades will disappear. Americans will not have to tolerate drug gangs—like New York City's Wild Cowboys, whose eight leaders, mostly from Dominican Republic, were convicted in 1995 of killing 10 people and of assaulting more than two dozen others, including rival gang members, their own gang members, witnesses, and bystanders.[7] Americans forgot the Capone gang, the O'Banion gang, and the Dutch Schultz gang after the repeal of alcohol prohibition. So too will fade from our memories such latter day gangs as the Wild Cowboys, the Gangster Disciples, the Crips, and the Bloods, after the repeal of drug prohibition.

Legalization will be no panacea. The United States will still have a problem with drug abusers and with a considerable number of miserable human beings who become addicted. Many of these drug users will carry on reasonably well in society despite their addiction, as they do now, but other more dissolute addicts will still become frightening to their families and friends, and just plain frustrating to community officials who must care for the social damage they create. Drug use will remain a burden for society. However, the biggest change Americans will notice is that the shooting and violence from rivals in drug trafficking—sometimes even from anti-drug enforcement—will be gone from our streets. Best of all, kids will not have to carry guns to school to protect themselves from rivals in other drug gangs.

The Enemy Is Us

Drug control in the peace that follows the drug war.

The Administration and Congress should realign our drug fighting forces by enacting legislation for an all-out attack against the demand for psychoactive drugs. Recent years have brought increasing recognition that the War on Drugs must concentrate on the demand side, even though our national leaders are unwilling to move far from supply-side suppression. Chapter 7 describes anti-drug projects in Albuquerque, NM, and Atlanta, GA, and among American Indian tribes. A recent Cronkite Report, on the Discovery television channel, described prevention projects in Indianapolis and the state of Arizona.. Walter Cronkite also described DTAP (Drug Treatment Alternative to Prison) in Brooklyn, NY, with a 16% rearrest rate as against a 40% rate for prison time. Fifty similar "drug courts" exist in some 30 states, while 50 more are planned, according to the National Association of Drug Court Professionals.[8] Legal officials have come to recognize that jail time is inappropriate for the "victimless crime" of drug use. Why should police and courts be involved at all? Why not simply encourage drug users to seek help? According to the Cronkite Report, the RAND Corporation "think tank" calculates that $1 for drug treatment is more productive than $7 for imprisonment.[9]

Coincident with actions that return all drugs to the legitimate private sector, the government should orchestrate a massive counter-advertising offensive against substance abusers within our society. It is important to maintain the integrity of these counter-advertising programs by being scrupulously factual, and to avoid the gross exaggerations that have marred previous government pronouncements on psychoactive drugs. The Partnership for a Drug Free America has enlisted leading advertising personnel in a campaign called "My Block, My Family." Tax revenue from legal drugs should be used to expand this and other such campaigns. Prevention programs would lead the attack, and treatment programs would be the mopping-up action. Many of the government employees from the drug enforcement agencies could hopefully transition into prevention and treatment organizations, both public and private. Government drug agents would probably be good candidates for positions in paramilitary drug rehabilitation camps for incorrigible addicts

Americans will wonder what they feared so much to have put themselves through the hell that this country endured with illegal drugs—all because of a mistaken belief that the prohibition of drugs would eliminate their use. The new experience will be like this nation's earlier experience with legal narcotics and cocaine—not nearly so disruptive, or damaging, as under prohibition. Our experience with alcohol prohibition demonstrated that corruption, crime, violence, and contempt for the law are the major byproducts of prohibition, and we have seen that axiom confirmed under drug prohibition.

Finding common ground for drug warriors and reformers

Dr. Gabriel G. Nahas has led an impassioned attack against cocaine use with his pharmacological assessment of cocaine's effects upon humans. From his perspective, "Man's future is threatened by this drug."[10] That frightening consequence is difficult to accept, knowing that the chewing of coca leaves has prevailed for over 2000 years, and cocaine was isolated over 130 years ago. But there is full agreement with his concern that we must not trivialize psychoactive drugs. Nahas wants a return to the pioneering example of Theodore Roosevelt, who, he believes, checked the opium epidemic at the turn of the century.[11] However, as was discussed in Chapter 3, a downturn in drug use was indicated long before any restrictive laws were ever passed. The moral temperament of pre-Progressive American society and its intolerance toward drug addiction accomplished a continuing reduction in substance abuse without any assistance from drug laws. Another paradox is that the greatest rise in illegal drug use occurred in America during the 1960s, shortly after the passage in 1956 of punitive anti-drug laws that even authorized the death penalty for the sale of heroin to minors.[12]

Nahas and others credit the dramatic drop-off in drug use in the 1920s and 1930s to a restrictive drug control policy, with minimal educational or medical intervention. Yet a restrictive alcohol control policy had little effect in stopping drinking during this period. A more probable cause for low drug use, rather than the restrictive controls, was young America's fascination with illegal booze, hip flasks, and speakeasies during alcohol prohibition. Surprisingly, during that period when American society flouted liquor prohibition, it continued its moral indignation toward drug use. Drug use remained a minor problem until well after the end of World War II.

Even that most restrictive drug control policy adopted in 1956 was of no help in containing the explosion in drug abuse in this country during the 1960s, when a change in social attitudes occurred and "turning-on" became in vogue. Societal attitudes and traditional morals are always a more dominant factor in the control of substance abuse than compulsory laws. When moral restraint is loosened—as it was in America in the 1960s, continuing up to the present day—restrictive drug laws will not stem the explosion in drug use. Cocaine use declined after the turn-of - the-century during the legal years and on into the prohibition years, becoming almost non-existent in the 1930s and 40s. But the most punitive drug laws in American history were ineffective in controlling the eruption of cocaine use by the "Yuppie" generation in the 1970s and 80s. Several times in his book Dr. Nahas acknowledges the greater power of moral persuasion in controlling drug use, but he still insists upon prohibition as the primary drug control despite its obvious failure.[13]

An overwhelming majority of Americans are opposed to recreational drug use, whether they support or oppose prohibition, and all are seeking the same end result—lower drug use. So how can we find common ground to work together toward our objective? Dr. Nahas states: "In order to stop the great white plague, the mass media, television, film, and press will have to start exerting, as they did in the past, a measure of restraint, and adopt towards illicit drug use a stand, at least as negative as the stand displayed against tobacco smoking or pollution of the environment. The glamorous and fashionable aspects of drug taking should no longer be favorably exposed on the movie or TV screen."[14] That is a statement on which most of us can agree. Developing a powerful social intolerance to recreational drug use is a necessity and a good starting point of agreement for all the soldiers in this War on Drugs.

In considering the position of notable drug warriors like William Bennett, James Q. Wilson, Mathea Falco, Gabriel Nahas, Joseph Califano, and practically all supporters of drug prohibition, we see that they share the goal to reduce drug use in this country to the greatest extent possible. We all, both prohibitionists and reformers, agree that demand-reduction programs are vital. We are also generally compatible in our views as to how drug reduction should be accomplished. Our difference is on the question from which platform should the United States launch its drug-reduction programs—drug prohibition or legalization? We have tried prohibition for over 75 years and have attempted suppression of the drug supply as the primary tool of enforcement. By every standard it has been a miserable failure. Now it is time for the prohibitionists to join in the movement for a change in policy and return to the private sector for a stable platform from which to launch our new anti-drug policy.

A society like grandpa's—with legal drugs

Was American society less moral than today during its first 144 years when all drugs were legal? Hardly. Drug addiction was considered an intolerable human condition in that society, and most people had even less tolerance for drunkards—an intolerance which inspired Americans to try prohibition So what will the United States be like in the new era without drug prohibition? Will legitimate drug markets reduce crime on our streets? History tells us it should. The United States had little drug related-crime when all drugs were legal.

There is a perceived notion by some that drugs cause people to commit crimes. Actually the relationship, rather than one of cause and effect, is symbiotic. Perpetrators of two immoral acts—drug use and drug selling—depend on each other to survive. Also, an influence on related drug and crime statistics stems from the fact that persons with criminal personalities are more likely than law-abiding persons to travel with the crowd that traffics in and abuses drugs. Regarding the question of drugs and violence, Dr. Musto makes an interesting observation: "One of the authorities in America who consistently tried to put narcotics and alcohol into perspective was Dr. Lawrence Kolb, Sr., of the Public Health Service in the 1920s. He liked to quote the British writer on inebriety Norman Kerr, who said in the late 19th century, 'Whiskey maddens man, while opium soothes him.' Kolb had his own saying that there was more violence in a gallon of alcohol than in a ton of opium."[15]

Legalization will not rid our society of all the criminals preying on the weak or unwary, but one-third to a half of all criminal convictions and incarcerations are currently drug-related. Prisons are now overflowing with drug offenders, resulting in many early releases of violent criminals back onto our streets. Legalization will free up resources in local police departments to concentrate on criminals who commit violent acts against other persons. Without the prison population of drug offenders we will be better able to remove the "bad actors" from society. Remember that we used to throw people in jail for selling and transporting alcohol.

The Enemy Is Us

Anyone studying the author's strategy for an anti-drug program would probably have something to add or subtract, or would approach the objective in a different way. Yet the crucial point is that Congress has not seriously reconsidered the wisdom of drug prohibition in over 75 years—even after the failure of alcohol prohibition and after the explosion in drug use in the last 30 years. There is no respectable advocate for recreational drug use, and every politician wants to stand up against it. Fine! Almost everyone agrees about the nation's objective; the disagreement is about the strategy to reach it. It is time to have a full debate on this subject.

The Objective for the Nation in Reducing Drug Use.

Earlier there was mention of an address by Dr. William L. Roper, Director, Centers for Disease Control, entitled, "Linking Science, Policy and Practice."[16] That address was presented to a professional conference on AIDS prevention; however, his words and recommendations can easily be applied to drug-use prevention. Since the Centers for Disease Control would be a major participant in any expanded public health program to prevent drug use, it is appropriate to refer to his following thoughts on prevention:

> ...It is, in fact, tempting to say that prevention's time has come. More than ever before we are positioned to deliver on our promise of a better life through disease prevention and health promotion. But to realize this promise, public health is going to have to provide genuine, vigorous leadership—not just within our own relatively narrow spheres of professional influence but for society as a whole.
>
> If we are really to be the leaders for prevention, I suggest that we all need to shed a few layers of protective timidity, to emerge from that comfortable corner in which we talk mostly to each other. We need, in short, to address the big issues on the main stage where societal decisions are made.

Your author shares Dr. Roper's insight that prevention, rather than prohibition, takes true courage. This outstanding official goes on to discuss the national campaign against smoking, which this book has cited as a model for the War on Drugs:

> It is useful to look to precedent when venturing into perilous waters, and fortunately here we have some—cases in which

154

public health has come out fighting on major social issues. One which is recent enough to be within our professional experience and is still continuing, is the case of Public Health v. Tobacco.

In January of 1964, now nearly 30 years ago, a public health David took on an industrial Goliath. When Surgeon General Luther Terry issued his first Report on Smoking and Health, the cigarette was a national symbol of all that is smart and sophisticated. Humphrey Bogart would never leave home, and certainly never be seen on the screen, without one. The Marlboro Man was the soul of manhood. Few indeed were the public places free of tobacco smoke—somebody else's smoke if not your own.

Moreover, the tobacco industry was second only to automobile manufacturers, and indeed a close second, in advertising and public relations expenditures. It controlled the economies of several states, and swung an even more powerful weight in the Congress than it does today.

Against this awesome monster, public health had just one missile for its sling—the truth. We used this weapon modestly. The most inflammatory sentence in the original Surgeon General's Report read: "Cigarette smoking is a health hazard of sufficient importance in the United States to warrant appropriate remedial action." It's the only sentence in the 387-page report printed in bold face type.

It doesn't seem like much today. Nowhere was there even a hint of what "appropriate remedial action" might be. Yet it made the front page of every major daily paper and the lead item in every newscast.

Your author is convinced that the media would give even more attention to the health hazard of recreational drugs. After all, such substances would lack the huge vested interests that support tobacco. Dr. Roper continues:

The fact is that "appropriate remedial action" is still unfolding, nearly three decades later, more and more each year. Meanwhile what has happened is a truly remarkable success story. We tend to forget that. We are impatient because the malady lingers on.

But literally millions of people are alive today because public health leadership did what it did. Millions are alive because public health extracted truth from science and courageously used it, unrelentingly over years, to alter public policy and influence individual and social behavior.

What has happened, with gathering force over the years, is a drastic change not only in individual lifestyles but also in social norms. Smokers are increasingly furtive; anti-smoking voices increasingly dominant. The ashtray is following the spittoon into oblivion. And all this is happening, not only because of the impact of education on individuals, but also as a result of a succession of social and economic events—enactment and enforcement of clean indoor air laws, raising taxes on cigarette purchases, the pressure on businesses to provide smoke-free environments for their employees and clientele.

...that, for my money, is "linking science, policy and practice." That's what we ought to be all about.

Some day these words in Dr. Roper's speech will surely be applied to the War on Drugs: "...public health extracted truth from science and courageously used it, unrelentingly over years, to alter public policy and influence individual and social behavior." This phrase stands out as the essence of this book's *Objective for the Nation in Reducing Drug Use*. He is right about prevention, and the United States should apply his principles by linking science, policy, and practice in the prevention and treatment of drug addiction. It is time to bring America's best minds together in working sessions, with open-minded determination to link these three disciplines together in the prevention of drug use.

Our *Objective for the Nation in Reducing Drug Use* encourages the practice of "accepting responsibility" by each citizen, and attempts to persuade each individual to exercise sound judgment for his or her own welfare and for the good of the community. Responsibility can be taught, and instilled in a society by community leaders who insist upon good civil discipline. This is a quality that has been diminishing in our society over the past 30 years, and the nation is struggling to reestablish civil obedience, responsibility, and respect for authority.

The U.S. government tried to legislate the desired behavior in the case of alcohol, narcotics, and cocaine by decreeing abstinence through prohibition. A proper and better course of action would have been to establish consequences for improper behavior by anyone under the influence of these substances, and to intervene only if personal conduct became detrimental to society or to other persons. Congress could have enacted legislation in 1914 that would have established persuasive regulations to discourage use of alcohol, narcotics, cocaine, etc. Dr. Roper has given us a perfect example in the government's approach to cigarette smoking. It was not prohibited, but over the years government-led program of health education, accompanied by restrictions on where, when, and how one could smoke, has given us a steady reduction in cigarette smoking. A national education program can begin by educating youth with the truth about what harm drugs do to one's mind and body, while avoiding the exaggerations and scare tactics that characterized the early days of the Federal Narcotics Bureau.

Try persuasion

There comes to mind a fable from the author's second-grade reader about the Sun and the Wind. They were arguing about which of the two was the more powerful, when they saw a solitary traveler wearing a great cloak, walking along the road.

"Look," said the Wind, "to settle this argument, let us see which of us can remove his cloak."

"Very well," replied the Sun, "you may try first," and the Sun moved behind a cloud. The Wind began to blow, but he had no effect. So he blew harder and harder, but the man only pulled his cloak tighter around himself.

Finally exhausted, the Wind said, "I give up, there is no way to remove his cloak."

"Let me try," said the Sun, as he came out from behind the cloud and brought his warm rays to bear upon the traveler. Soon the man began to perspire, and feeling warm, removed his cloak and carried it on his arm.

The implied moral to the story is that persuasion can often be more effective than force. This was a moral taught to me in the second grade and never forgotten. If we teach morals and traditional values to children, some will ignore them when they are adults, but none will forget them. As long as people remember moral lessons, most can be influenced to avoid the pitfalls of the world. After three-quarters of a century under the brute force of prohibition, we can safely conclude that it is not going to work, so now it is time to try moral persuasion.

The Enemy Is Us

Bugler, sound the charge!

Let the battle be joined. The hard-liners who have maintained this nation's failed drug policy are about to be exposed in their law enforcement fortress and prohibition overturned. There is no enemy but ourselves, and Americans can better resolve their drug-use problem without the fear and panic created by the law enforcement bureaucrats. Their draconian measures have spread death, violence, and corruption across our land without reducing drug use. Every aspect of America's drug problem has been exacerbated under prohibition, and another 75 years will not be enough time to make this failed program work. Armed with only the truth, the forces for a change in drug policy can overcome the prevailing misconceptions of the public about the value of prohibition.

The forces for a change in drug policy have, up to this point been fragmented and unable to offer a cohesive plan of action for the population to rally around. There are many adherents for change, but they consist of splinter groups, each pursuing its own limited agenda. The Drug Policy Foundation has created an umbrella under which all groups may gather and exchange ideas. The members take great pleasure in small victories on the periphery, such as the easing of a state drug law or a court decision that eases the penalty for a drug user. Much like the United Nations, the foundation is great forum but has been short on developing a bold strategy to slay the prohibition dragon. The author presents this book's plan as a rallying point around which every adherent for change will find his particular concern to be satisfied. It is also the only way to eliminate illegal drug trafficking and all of its evils.

The rallying cry is "Repeal drug prohibition." We must spread the word and continue the frontal assault on the fortress of prohibition. The defenders of the fortress are the drug enforcement bureaucracies—the same forces that America set against the drug cartels. Yet, without prohibition there would be no worldwide drug syndicate to fight, and the enforcers' bureaucratic fiefdom would fall. If the forces for change become organized, and remain focused, we will attract millions to the cause. This ground swell of public opinion for change will provide cover for the Congressional leaders to move in and remove the bulwarks of the prohibition bureaucracy. Congress needs the assurance of public backing before it will move for repeal. The situation can change rapidly and now is the time to press the attack. The Drug Enforcement Agency will counter by pointing to the recent capture of drug cartel leaders and to the tons of cocaine seized. But the focus should be kept on the amount of drugs on our streets and the number of children being destroyed by this drug war.

It takes great political courage for an elected member of Congress to take a stand contrary to the public's popularly held opinion and to rebut bureaucratic misinformation. But America has always had leaders who, when armed with the truth, would stand up to overturn an injustice. The author believes that there are leaders in Congress, today, who will step forward to lead the United States out of the drug policy morass. America is counting on them.

10

DISPATCH TO THE COMMANDER IN CHIEF

Note to the reader: This chapter is addressed to William Clinton, President of the U.S.A. as this book is being written. But it is addressed equally to anyone who seeks, or wins, the office of Chief Executive of our nation until drug prohibition is ended. Under the American system of government, as the reader knows, Congress makes the nation's laws. The President, however, is expected to define a national strategy and to show leadership in mobilizing support for that strategy. No action is more crucial to a successful national strategy than repeal of laws prohibiting the production, sale, and consumption of any psychoactive drug.

Mr. President, it is recommended that you address the nation to relate your plan for an organized approach to create a new drug policy. It is the consensus of the American people that there is no matter of greater urgency to the United States than a speedy resolution to the problem of illegal drugs and crime. These two problems exist in a symbiotic relationship, where each nourishes the other's growth. The forces for a New Drug Policy offer this book's Battle Plan as a strategy to destroy that relationship and eliminate drug trafficking while greatly reducing crime.

In your deliberations over the New Battle Plan, please consider the following:

• Liberty is America's greatest heritage.

• Freedom to make a personal choice, in absence of harm to another, is our most cherished right.

• A free enterprise system is the economic foundation of this nation.

• The Bill of Rights is the protector of the citizen from government tyranny.

Drug prohibition has eroded the value of all four of these principles and is a threat to destroy them entirely. Drug prohibition fathered illegal drug trafficking, which is the catalyst for the cancer spreading through our society in the form of crime, violence, corruption, and incarcerations. That cancer is eroding our liberty. It is not just the mean streets of our cities that our citizens are avoiding. Americans are often in fear of venturing on main street. Our citizens are constantly being threatened or killed by the cross-fire from rival drug gangs and even from police shoot-outs with drug dealers. Participants from all sides of the drug war are using assault weapons.

Drug smugglers disrupt our nation's commerce by using legitimate businesses as conduits for their drugs and to hide their bloated profits. Drug dealers flood the banking system with millions of dollars in illegal cash, and the drug cartels corrupt the monetary system with their money-laundering schemes. The estimated value of illegal drug sales is over $100 billion annually and constitutes the largest part of our nation's underground economy, which pays no taxes. Not only does this illegal enterprise avoid taxes, it corrupts our public officials and every institution in this country.

Juvenile drug gangs have spread out from their neighborhoods to cover entire cities. They have moved into small towns across the United States, organizing and sponsoring local youths in the illegal drug business. Every customer that they can convert also becomes a potential drug seller. In this manner, these drug gangs pyramid their sales forces into a powerful instrument for spreading drug addiction across our nation. ABC television network news' investigations into juvenile drug gangs reported an alarming picture. One gang in Chicago, "the Gangster Disciples," has over 30,000 members with subordinate gangs in 150 towns. The Gangster Disciples are controlled by a drug dealer, Larry Hoover, from a prison cell where he is serving time. In addition to their illegal activities, this gang utilizes its members as active participants in a political activist group called "21st Century Vote." Their primary purpose is to sponsor local candidates that will be sympathetic to their illegal enterprise, but they also participate in civic get-out-the-vote drives.[1] These kinds of activities, involving that many gang members, can corrupt the entire elective process of a city.

Our nation's attempts to eliminate or reduce the use of illegal drugs are met by ever more elaborate and sophisticated schemes of the drug cartels to smuggle their contraband. They have gone from slipping through a kilo or two of heroin or cocaine, with a lone courier, to transporting tons of drugs, mingled with legal cargo. The size and scope of the illegal drug enterprise is adversely impacting legitimate commerce in the United States.

The Enemy Is Us

Our government's frustration with the continued growth of this underworld activity has caused our legislative branch to enact extreme penalties against participants. It has also placed expensive reporting requirements on business in the hope of ferreting out illegal acts. The RICO Act may have been upheld by the Supreme Court, but it authorizes seizure of private property without due process. This law received the approval of the Court and the American people because it targeted the despised drug dealers. However, it has also been applied against Right-to-Life groups protesting abortion, and you can be assured the criminal justice system will find other unlikely situations where it can apply this law. Using seizure laws to enforce drug prohibition will continue to wear away the Constitutional rights of Americans. Prohibition itself denies an American, in the absence of harm to another, the right to make a personal choice to use or not to use a drug. This danger to individual liberty is being recognized, albeit slowly, when, as mentioned in Chapter 5, a federal appeals court ruled against the practice of seizing a defendant's property in a civil court proceeding if the defendant is also being prosecuted in criminal court. Congress has also recognized this peril, and Rep. Henry Hyde, R. IL, has introduced a bill to stop property confiscations when there has been no conviction.

As mentioned earlier, the United Nations Development Report of 1994 tells us that the retail value of illegal drugs now exceeds international trade in oil and is second only to the arms trade. Can the world community allow any commodity, with trade of that magnitude, to remain in the exclusive domain of international criminals? The United States has vigorously pursued a policy of coercion and armed intervention for 75 years to eliminate drug crops and drug trafficking in source nations, while drug use in America continued to expand. It is not a question of whether we can win a drug war against organized crime; rather it is a question of why should we engage in armed conflict with drug traffickers at all. We can eliminate them without firing a shot by bringing all drugs into the domain of legal world trade, and simultaneously reduce drug use in America.

The United States was the instigator and the driving force in organizing the nations of the world to stamp out opium use, and later, use of other drugs. We Americans were putting pressure on the source countries to destroy the drug crops and to control trafficking. That idea, at best, has not worked out well. Our former leaders in the United States led the world into this drug quagmire, but now it is time to acknowledge our faulty strategy and show the world a way out. We can learn from our mistakes and successes over this century to develop a thoughtful drug policy. We can reestablish a legitimate and private drug business for production, distribution, and consumption of narcotics and cocaine in the United States without involving or depending on any other nation. Mr. President, this is your moment on the world stage. This is your opportunity to reshape our drug policy to resolve a problem that has plagued our nation and the world for decades. Don't be bound by the drug phobia that paralyzes most political leaders, but act boldly.

Look to your personal experience, Mr. President.

In the last Presidential campaign you stated your adamant opposition to the legalization of drugs. You elaborated by saying that if drugs had been legal your brother, Roger, would not be alive today. One can understand your stated opposition to drug legalization. No politician waging a campaign in today's environment wants to be labeled as "soft" on drugs. But it is difficult to rationalize how the legalization of drugs would have caused your brother's death. There has been a glut of cocaine and heroin on the market in the past twenty years and these drugs could not have been more available if they had been legal. Using and dealing in illegal drugs put Roger at greater risk of death from the drug dealers. There was also the risk of death from adulterated drugs, or even being killed accidentally by the drug enforcement authorities. If you mean his arrest and imprisonment separated him from drugs, surely we can find ways in a legitimate drug environment to isolate drug abusers from drugs without imprisoning addicts with violent criminals. Explain to us why you feel that leaving the manufacturing, distributing, and selling of drugs in the hands of hoodlums and murderers is better than having legitimate pharmaceutical houses and pharmacies perform these functions.

Roger Clinton's behavior was unwise, but if he had lived during any of the administrations from George Washington to Woodrow Wilson, his actions would not have been criminal. Mr. President, think about the hell this country is going through trying to keep a small part of our population from self-destructive behavior. Can you not recognize that we can deal with the folly of individual drug use and addiction more effectively if we eliminate the criminals, murderers, corrupters, and profiteers from this hellish situation? Legal and freely available

163

narcotics and cocaine will not stimulate an increase in addiction rates. Cheap, legal, and freely available drugs are exactly what we had in this nation for most of our history. Even in that environment, Theodore Roosevelt's administration was able to put addiction rates in decline by educating the public to this danger. During his Presidency, Congress required drug corporations to list contents on the label of their medications, and our government helped to create a social intolerance to the irresponsible behavior of recreational drug use.

Remember, Mr. President, that the addiction rates, on a per capita basis, before the Harrison Narcotics Act of 1914, using the most acceptable statistics available, were less than a third of today's rate. And just as remarkable, drug crime was almost non-existent. After the Harrison Narcotics Act, America had legal narcotics and cocaine for the next five years by doctor's prescription only. The IRS law enforcers obtained complete prohibition by 1920, and since then we have had both a drug and a crime problem. Fortunately, Roger Clinton was able to rehabilitate himself, but he was not the only hapless soul caught in this web of deceit and corruption. The thrill of a short, euphoric high, or the lure of huge profits, has tempted many to join the drug subculture. Drug pushing isn't confined only to the inner-city streets. Drug salespersons are recruited from all walks of life and might be anyone from the preacher's daughter to the Surgeon General's son. The star undercover agent of the DEA in Miami was recently arrested for withholding $700,000 that he had picked up in a drug laundering sting operation. Several of our young Coast Guard members and countless police officers have been apprehended for dealing in drugs. No one seems to be immune from the many temptations of illegal drugs lying in wait for the weak or unwary. They have corrupted our entire nation.

No one has yet proposed a strategy that will take the underworld out of the business of supplying these illegal substances, other than returning this business to the domain of legitimate commerce. All of your administration's programs to reduce the demand for illegal drugs are compromised and hindered by drug dealers constantly creating new addicts and reclaiming old addicts after their rehabilitation. Drug dealers are constantly recruiting foolish people to do their bidding for expected big bucks and a quick payoff. It happened with alcohol as it is happening with drugs. No city or state in the United States can resolve its drug problem unless Congress changes the federal drug control policy. Crime associated with the illegal drug trade is a greater problem than individual addictions. Mr. President, it is time to acknowledge the failure of our federal drug control policy and to talk about drug legalization.

Placing nicotine and alcohol under the drug control umbrella

Can social abhorrence and disapproval of recreational drug use (including alcohol and nicotine) be raised to a level where we will see a steady decline in the use of these substances? Can we markedly improve the general health of our population? Yes, but it will take a well thought out campaign and the leadership that you could give it, Mr. President.

President George Bush demonstrated that kind of leadership in marshaling the forces of the world in the Desert Storm operation. He articulated the necessity of this operation to the American people in a way that won him overwhelming public support. He prodded a timid United Nations into action, and finally cajoled a recalcitrant Congress to vote their support for his proposed action. Then his team executed a masterful battle plan to win a miraculous victory in only three days.

We can do the same thing in preventing drug use—not in three days, but probably in less time than we have taken with cigarette smoking. It took more than fifty years for our government to acknowledge that we had a smoking and health problem, then another thirty-years to get to the point we are today—where we are about to bring smoking under control. It may take a generation to bring drug use down to the point where it is no longer a significant problem, but we need to start that steady, continuous reduction in drug use now.

Drug legalization will bring almost immediate relief from the crime, violence, drug killings, corruption, and prison overcrowding that we identify as our "drug problem." We will immediately see less violence on our streets, the disappearance of drug dealers, and a reduced demand for the weapons that juvenile gangs carry to protect their drug enterprise. The prison population will drop by a third or more. The country will quickly develop a positive feeling about the situation, like the relief that the repeal of alcohol prohibition brought to the nation in 1933.

This nation should learn something from the repeal of alcohol prohibition in 1933. There was a much greater percentage of the population drinking during prohibition than we have using drugs today. A celebration attitude greeted repeal and the alcohol industry quickly swung into action, advertising and promoting their products. Drug legalization will bring relief that the drug war is finally over. Yet with that relief should come a sober reflection and a cautious concern, rather than celebration. We can manage drug legalization better than alcohol legalization by not permitting advertising, or sales promotion. Much will still need to be done. Working with our addict population will require patience and persistence, but the greatest effort must be given to drug education and prevention. There will be shock to some when they see packets labeled COCAINE or HEROIN, just as bottles of liquor on display were shocking to many after repeal. But pharmacists dispensing heroin and cocaine will soon take on an air of normalcy and we can concentrate on guiding our youth instead of blaming the drug dealers.

Listen to the voice of the people

The voices of the people are calling for a new action. Once a dialogue begins, and minds are open to finding a better solution, the experience of our past, plus common sense, will lead to the repeal of drug prohibition. When legitimate businesses control the manufacture, distribution, and sale of what are now illicit drugs, there will be no room for the overseas drug cartels, the drug dealers, or the street drug pushers. Once you, Mr. President, are convincingly behind the repeal of drug prohibition, your drug-fighting bureaucracy will fall into line and begin to scramble for positions in the realigned organizations for drug prevention and treatment. Peace will be declared in the War on Drugs, and the drug-fighting bureaucracy will fight the drug problem with a new weapon—truth. Truth will be broadcast about the harm drugs do to the user, about ways to avoid being deceived into drug use, and about the benefits of leading a life free of substance dependency. Drug avoidance now becomes a health and medical issue, and this is where the tax revenues from drug sales should be directed. The nation will spend the greater part of our substance abuse prevention and treatment budget in the Department of Health and Human Resources.

One goal is to relieve society of the financial burden of caring for the drug-disabled users. Mr. President, we can finance their care, treatment, or confinement in medical and correctional institutions with tax revenues from legal drug sales. Federal drug taxes can be conservatively estimated at one-fifth of the value of current illegal drug sales, or $20 billion annually. The United States' budget deficit will greatly improve with this new revenue flowing to our treasury, rather than going as drug profits to the drug cartels. The federal, state, and municipal governments will save an estimated $40 billion now spent to enforce the drug ban.

Americans want so keenly to do something about their drug problem that we have deluded ourselves into thinking that overseas drug lords are the enemy, and that by eliminating them we will somehow have solved our dilemma. If we were to succeed in eliminating the drug cartels, drug suppliers in another form would soon appear to fill the needs of the American drug user. But, Mr. President, you should tell this truth about the War on Drugs—the enemy is not overseas. We Americans are our own worst enemy. So let us redirect our attack on the enemy at home.

CONCLUSION
The reader's responsibility

This book is written for all persons interested in reducing drug use in this nation. The hope is that the ideas presented will stimulate the reader's thinking on possible solutions to the drug problem. We may have some differences in our proposed solutions, but we are all working toward the same objective—to find a more effective policy to reduce psychoactive drug use within our society.

An exchange of ideas and a constructive debate should lead to a better drug policy for the nation. The Battle Plan presented in this book is validated by empirical evidence from America's past and present experiences. The author believes it will accomplish our objective. The reader may have better ideas. Your ideas and plan should do nothing less than the following:

- Reduce drug use within the general population.
- Eliminate the crime, violence, killings, guns, corruption, and incarcerations surrounding drug sales.
- Provide funds and a method to prevent or treat drug addiction.

The War on Drugs is conducted for the purpose of cutting off the supply of drugs, but the glut of illegal drugs on our streets is direct evidence that America's efforts are not working and has never worked. The War on Drugs should end immediately. Not only will we have saved the money and lives expended in that fight, we also will have eliminated the illegal drug money that is corrupting our courts, judicial officials, law enforcement officials, customs agents, correction officials, banking officers, and even our young men of the Coast Guard. Drug money has stained every institution in the country, from Congress to the courthouse. Illegal drug money is responsible for much of the breakdown in the moral fiber of our society in the past 32 years. Once the criminal element is removed from the drug trade, our prevention and treatment programs can become effective in a systematic reduction of drug use in our society. Ridding our society of the cynicism and hypocrisy associated with drug prohibition will allow the renewal of America to begin.

There must be a national moral renewal as well as a change in laws, if substance abuse is to be eliminated as a major societal problem.

168

Conclusion

Fortunately there is a movement toward moral renewal in the U.S.A. The conservative Christian Coalition has called for such renewal in its "Contract with the American Family." The contract states: "The American people are increasingly concerned about the coarsening of our culture, the breakup of the family and a decline in civility." A large group of liberal Christian leaders differs with many of the Contract's particulars but agrees with its general diagnosis. The liberals call their statement "The Cry for Renewal."[1] Your author devoutly hopes that liberal and conservative Christians—as well as members of other churches and the unchurched—can resolve their differences and agree on a program of moral renewal.

Stephen Covey best expressed the thought your author wishes to convey when he said: "I believe that there are parts to human nature that cannot be reached by either legislation or education, but require the power of God to deal with. I believe that as human beings, we cannot perfect ourselves. To the degree to which we align ourselves with correct principles, divine endowments will be released within our nature in enabling us to fulfill the measure of our creation."[2] Americans should remember that the Judeo-Christian ethic was the foundation of this nation, and that the drug problem is only one of the symptoms of the breakdown in morals, ethics, and character that our country has been experiencing. Abraham Lincoln reinforced the principles upon which this nation was founded, when he stated, "Those nations only are blessed whose God is the Lord."

Here is the author's challenge to every reader: You have demonstrated your interest in America's drug problem by reading this book. Now, demonstrate your responsibility as a citizen and further inform yourself of the facts about our present drug policy. Next, evaluate this information from a dispassionate and realistic perspective. Finally, express your feelings to your representative in Congress, your Senators, and the President. Urge their action in opening hearings and starting the debate to find an alternative for our present failed drug policy. If we the people fail to do our duty—by personal example and by political action—in the War on Drugs, we shall be forced to say with Pogo, "The enemy is us."

BIBLIOGRAPHY

Books

Allen, David Franklin and Jekel, James F.., *Crack: the broken promise*, New York: St. Martin's Press, 1991

Allen, Frederick Lewis, *Only Yesterday: An Informal History of the Nineteen-Twenties,* New York: Bantam, 1957 (orig. publ. by Harper & Brothers, 1931).

Bartimole, Carmella and John, *Teenage Alcoholism and Substance Abuse: Causes, Cures and Consequences.* New York: Frederick Fell Publishers, 1987.

Benjamin, Daniel K. and Miller, Roger LeRoy, *Undoing Drugs: Beyond Legalization.* New York: Basic Books, Division of Harper Collins, 1991.

Bernards, Neal, editor, *War on drugs: Opposing Viewpoints.* San Diego: Greenhaven Press, 1990.

Boaz, David, editor, *The Crisis in Drug Prohibition.* Washington, D.C.: The Cato Institute, 1990.

Brecher, Edward M. and the Editors of Consumer Reports, *Licit and Illicit Drugs.* Boston & Toronto: Little Brown, 1972.

Chatlos, Calvin, with Chilnick, Lawrence D., Crack: *What You Should Know about the Cocaine Epidemic*, New York: Perigee Books, The Putnam Publishing Group., 1987.

Cocores, James, *The 800-Cocaine Book of Drug and Alcohol Recovery*, New York: Fireside, 1991 (orig. publ. by Villard Books, 1990).

Coontz, Stephanie, *The Way We Never Were*, New York: Basic Books, Division of Harper Collins, 1992.

Courtwright, David T., *Dark Paradise: Opiate Addiction in America before 1940*, Cambridge, MA.: Harvard University Press, 1982.

Covey, Stephen R., *Seven Habits of Highly Effective People: Restoring the Character Ethic*, New York: Simon and Schuster, 1989.

Doyle, Charlotte L., *Explorations in Psychology*, Monterey, CA.: Brooks/Cole, 1987.

Falco, Mathea, *The Making of a Drug Free America, programs that work*, New York: Times Books, Division of Random House, 1992.

Bibliography

Friedman, Milton and Szasz, Thomas S., *On Liberty and Drugs*, edited and with a preface by Arnold S. Trebach and Kevin B. Zeese, Washington, D.C.: The Drug Policy Foundation Press, 1992.

Garraty, John A., *The American Nation*, New York: Harper and Row, 1966.

Gold, Mark S., *The Good News About Drugs and Alcohol: Curing, Treating, and Preventing Substance Abuse in the New age of Biopsychiatry*, New York: Villard Books, Division of Random House, 1991.

Hoobler, Thomas & Dorothy, Drugs and Crime: *The Encyclopedia of Psychoactive Drugs, Series 2*, New York: Chelsea House, 1988.

Holy Bible, King James Version

Lebergott, Stanley, *The Americans: An Economic Record*, New York: W. W. Norton, 1984.

Lee, Rensselaer W. III, *The White Labyrinth: Cocaine Trafficking and Political Power in the Andean Countries.* New Brunswick, NJ.: Transaction Publishers, A Foreign Policy Research Institute book, 1990.

Lender, Mark Edward and Martin, James Kirby, *Drinking In America: A History*, New York: The Free Press, Division of Macmillan, 1982.

Long, Robert Emmet, Editor, *Drugs in America, The Reference Shelf*, New York: H. W. Wilson, 1993.

McCoy, Alfred W., *The Politics of Heroin*, Brooklyn & Chicago: Lawrence Hill, 1991.

Miller, Richard Lawrence, *The Case For Legalizing Drugs*, New York: Praeger, an imprint of Greenwood Publishing Group, 1991.

Murray, Charles, *Losing Ground: American Social Policy, 1950-1980*, New York: Basic Books, 1984.

Musto, David F., *The American Disease: Origins of Narcotic Controls.* Expanded Edition. New York: Oxford University Press, 1987 (orig. publ. by Yale University Press, 1973.)

Nahas, Gabriel G., *Cocaine: the Great White Plague*, Middlebury, VT.: Paul S Eriksson, 1989.

Olasky, Marvin, *The Tragedy of American Compassion*, Wheaton, IL.: Crossway Books, division of Good News Publishers, 1992.

Roberts, Sam, *Who We Are: A Portrait of America Based on the Latest U.S. Census,* New York: Times Books, 1993.

Shannon, Elaine, *Desperados: Latin Drug Lords, U.S. Lawmakers and the War America Can't Win*, New York: Viking Press, 1988.

171

Bibliography

Taylor, Maxwell D., *The Uncertain Trumpet*, New York: Harper & Brothers, 1960.

Voy, Robert O., *Drugs, Sports and Politics*, Champaign, IL.:   Leisure Press, division of Human Kinetics, 1991.

Williams, Terry, *The Cocaine Kids, The Inside Story of a Teenage Drug Ring*, Reading, MA.: Addison-Wesley, 1989.

Articles

Allen, John, & Mazzuchi, John, Alcohol and Drugs Abuse among American Military Personnel: Prevalence and Policy Implications., *Military Medicine*, Vol. 150, May 1985, pp. 250-255.

Bennett, William, Should Drugs Be Legalized? *Readers Digest*, Mar. 1990, pp.90-94.

Benoit, Ellen & Coletti, Richard J., Drugs: the Case for Legalization, *Financial World*, Oct. 3, 1989, pp. 32-35.

Bray, R. M., Marsden, M. E., Peterson, M. R., Standardized Comparisons of the Use of Alcohol, Drugs and Cigarettes among Military Personnel and Civilians., *American Journal of Public Health.*, Vol. 81, July 1991, pp. 866-870.

Economist of London editors, Is Legalization the Answer? *World Press Review*, Nov. 1989, pp. 27-28.

Gardner, Lytt I. Jr., Substance Abuse in Military Personnel: Better or Worse? *American Journal of Public Health*, Vol. 81, July 1991, pp. 837-838.

Gazzaniga, Michael S., The Federal Drugstore, *National Review*, Feb. 5, 1990, pp. 34-41.

Hawley, Richard A., Legalizing the Intolerable is a Bad Idea, *Phi Delta Kappan*, Sep. 1991, pp 62-65.

Hess, John L , Just Say No?, *Present Tense*, Sept.-Oct. 1989, pp. 61-62.

Kagan, Daniel, How America Lost Its First Drug War., *Insight*, Nov. 30, 1989, pp. 65-74.

Miller, Mark, Unveiling Bennett's Battle Plan to Curb Drug-related Violence in Washington, *Newsweek*, Apr. 24, 1989.

Murray, Charles, How to Win the War on Drugs., *The New Republic*, May 21, 1990, pp. 19-24.

Murray, Charles, Drug Free Zones: Winning the War on Drugs, *Current*, Oct. 1990, pp. 19-25.

Bibliography

Musto, David F., Opium, Cocaine and Marijuana in American History, *Scientific American*, July 1991, pp. 40-47.

Nadelmann, Ethan A., Drug Prohibition in the United States: Costs, Consequences, and Alternatives., *Science*, Sep. 1, 1989, pp. 939-947.

Slaughter, James B., Marijuana Prohibition in the United States: History and Analysis of a Failed Policy., *Columbia Journal of Law and Social Problems*., Volume 21, Number 4, 1988, pp. 417-474.

Solzhenitsyn, Aleksandr, Men Have Forgotten God., *National Review*, July 22, 1983, pp.872-876.

Wilson, James Q., Against the Legalization of Drugs., *Commentary*, February 1990, pp.21-29.

Wink, Walter, Biting the Bullet: The Case for Legalizing Drugs, *The Christian Century*, Aug 8-15, 1990, pp. 736-739.

Government Publications

Bacon, John, The Federal Response to the United States Drug Problem 1960-1989. A Study Commissioned by Pennsylvania Governor William Donald Schaefer's Drug and Alcohol Abuse Commission, Harrisburg: December 1989.

Final Report, National Commission on Drug-Free Schools., September 1990.

Johnston, Lloyd D, O'Malley, P. M., & Bachman, J. G., National Survey Results on Drug Use from the Monitoring the Future study, 1975-1992 (Volume I: Secondary School Students). Rockville, MD.: National Institute on Drug Abuse, April 13, 1993.

National Household Survey on Drug Abuse: Population Estimates 1991, Revised, November 20, 1992.

Report to the President and the Attorney General, America's Habit: Drug Abuse, Drug Trafficking, and Organized Crime, 1986.

Timrots, Anita, Fact Sheet: Drug Use Trends, Washington, D.C.: Drugs & Crime Data Center & Clearinghouse., U.S. Department of Justice, May 1992.

Miscellaneous

Alcoholism: Life Under the Influence. One of a series of ten 1 hour Nova programs, produced by WGBH, Boston. Distributor: Ambrose Video Publishers, Inc. 1984.

Bibliography

Califano, Joseph A. Jr., and others, Legalization: Panacea or Pandora's Box, White Paper #1, Center on Addiction and Substance Abuse, Columbia University, New York, September 1995.

Newspapers—Numerous articles and reports relating to illegal drugs and drug controls.

Novello, Antonia C., Surgeon General, "Illegal Underage Drinking and Smoking," speech before the Texas Commission on Alcohol and Drug Abuse, July 13, 1992.

Roper, William L., Director, Centers for Disease Control, "Linking Science, Policy and Practice," speech before Prevention '92 Conference, March 24, 1992, Baltimore, Md.

Television—Numerous recorded interviews with public officials, public affair discussions, and news reports on the subject of illegal drugs and drug control.

NOTES

Note: See Bibliography for complete publishing information on books.

Chapter 1

[1] Pogo; a comic strip creation of the late Walt Kelly

[2] Musto, David F., Opium, Cocaine and Marijuana in American History, *Scientific American*, July 1991, p. 45.

[3] Califano, Joseph A. Jr., and others, Legalization: Panacea or Pandora's Box, White Paper #1, *Center on Addiction and Substance Abuse,* Columbia University, New York, September 1995.

[4] Kingdom of Cocaine, TV special report with Judy Woodruff, *Cable News Network,* September 25, 1994. CNN quoted the 1994 United Nations Development Report as stating that the retail value of the illegal drug trade is estimated at $500 billion, exceeding the international trade in oil and second only to the arms trade.

[5] If Drugs Were Legal, by Paul Harvey, *Prime Time,* Albuquerque, New Mexico, Distributed by Creators Syndicate, Inc., January 1995, p. 4.

[6] Legalize drugs or get tough on them, Gingrich urges, *The Miami Herald,* July 15, 1995, p. 3A

[7] Allen, Frederick Lewis, *Only Yesterday, An Informal History of the Nineteen Twenties*, 1931, pp. 257-258.

Chapter 2

[1] Musto, David F., Opium, Cocaine, and Marijuana in American History, *Scientific American*, July 1991, p. 42.

[2] Ibid., p. 43.

[3] Ibid., p. 43.

[4] Ibid., pp. 40-43.

[5] Musto, David F., *The American Disease*, 1987, p. 279, n. 2.

[6] Musto, David F., Opium, Cocaine, and Marijuana in American History, *Scientific American,* July 1991, p. 44.

[7] Nahas, Gabriel G., *Cocaine: The Great White Plague*, 1989, p. 41.

[8] Brecher, Edward M. & the Editors of Consumer Reports, *Licit and Illicit Drugs*, 1972, pp. 406-410.

NOTES

9 A Vin Mariana advertisement featuring contemporary celebrities, *Harper's Weekly Advertiser*, vol. 37, Oct.28, 1893.

10 Ibid.

11 Musto, Opium, Cocaine, and Marijuana in American History, p. 44.

12 Musto, *The American Disease*, p. 5.

13 Ibid., p. 42.

14 Lender, Mark Edward & Martin, James Kirby, *Drinking In America: A History,* 1982, pp. 35-37 & 46.

15 Ibid., pp. 64-68 & 95-96.

16 Garraty, John A., *The American Nation.* 1966, p. 705.

17 Brecher and others, Chs. 23 & 26.

18 Ibid., pp. 44 & 48.

19 Musto, *The American Disease*, p. 51.

20 Ibid., pp. 62-65.

21 Falco, Mathea, *The Making of a Drug-Free America--Programs That Work.* 1992, p. 20; and Brecher and others, ch. 56.

22 Lender and others, pp. 137-138; and, Allen, Frederick Lewis, *Only Yesterday: An Informal History of the Nineteen Twenties.* 1931, p. 267.

23 Hoobler, Thomas and Dorothy, *Drugs and Crime,* The Encyclopedia of Psychoactive Drugs, Series 2, 1988, p. 31.

24 Musto, *The American Disease*, p.184.

25 Ibid., p. 206.

26 Ibid., p. 193.

27 Ibid., pp. 190-191.

28 Ibid., p. 191.

29 Ibid., p. 191

30 Brecher and others, , pp. 13-14.

31 Goode, Erich, Drug Abuse, *Grolier's Electronic Encyclopedia*, 1993, pp. 13, 14.

32 Allen, p. 8.

33 Brecher and others, pp. 337-341, and 370-380.

34 Hoobler, p.15.

35 Brecher and others, pp. 291-292, and 416.

36 Goode, pp. 20-24.

NOTES

Chapter 3

[1] Musto, David F., *The American Disease, Origins of Narcotic Control*, 1987, p. 66.

[2] Musto, David F., Opium, Cocaine and Marijuana in American History, *Scientific American*, July 1991, p. 43.

[3] Ibid., p. 43.

[4] Opium Wars, *Academic American Encyclopedia*, 1994.

[5] Boxer Uprising, *Academic American Encyclopedia*, 1994.

[6] Musto, David F., Opium, Cocaine and Marijuana in American History, *Scientific American*, July 1991, p. 43.

[7] Ibid., p. 43.

[8] Ibid., pp. 43-44.

[9] Musto, David F., *The American Disease*, p. 292, n. 40.

[10] Ibid, p. 64

[11] Ibid., pp. 132, 133.

[12] Covey, Stephen R., *Seven Habits of Highly Effective People*, 1989, pp. 260, 284.

[13] Alcohol prohibition was enacted by the Volstead Act of 1919, after passage of the 18th Amendment to the Constitution. Narcotics and cocaine became illegal after a Supreme Court ruling, in 1919, held that the Harrison Act of 1914 prohibited administering narcotics for addiction maintenance, even by a doctor's prescription.

[14] Rich, Spencer, Are Old Habits Going Up in Smoke?, *The Washington Post Weekly*, January 9-15, 1995.

[15] The passage of the 21st Amendment to the Constitution, in 1933, repealed the prohibition of alcohol.

[16] Harvey, Paul, We're Killing Ourselves!, *Prime Time*, Albuquerque, NM, March 1995, p. 4. Paul Harvey was quoting from a 1993 article in the government journal Alcohol Health and Research World, in which Dr. Dorothy Rice of the University of California has compiled the economic costs of alcoholism.

[17] Donald Mabry, a scholar at Mississippi State University, testifying before Congress, The Defense Monitor, Center for Defense Information, Vol. XXI, Number 1, 1992, p. 2.

[18] Nahas, Gabriel G., *Cocaine: the Great White Plague*, 1989.

[19] Gold, Mark S., *The Good News About Drugs and Alcohol: Curing, Treating and Preventing Substance Abuse in the New Age of Biopsychiatry*, 1991.

NOTES

[20] Nahas, p. 72.

[21] Musto, *The American Disease*, p. 42. Information gathered in Wright's national survey indicated that among physicians, about 2 percent and among nurses, about 1 percent were habitués of some form of opium. Only 0.7 percent of other professional classes and 0.2 percent of the general population were addicted. The United States' population in 1910 was 91,972,266.

[22] Falco, Mathea, *The Making of a Drug Free America--Programs That Work*, 1992, pp 11 & 223, n. 25.

[23] ABC Evening News with Peter Jennings, February 8,1995.

[24] *The Miami Herald*, Tuesday, January 30, 1995, p.10A.

[25] Olasky, Marvin, *The Tragedy of American Compassion*, 1992, p. 233.

[26] My father's house has many mansions, *The Washington Post National Weekly Edition*, Sept 11-17, 1995, p. 8.

Chapter 4

[1] Nadelmann, Ethan A., Drug Prohibition in the United States: Costs, Consequences, and Alternatives., 1 Sept 1989, *Science*, vol. 245, pp. 939-946. Also, Wharton Economic Forecasting Associates, *The Impact: Organized Crime Today* (President's Commission on Organized Crime, Washington, DC, 1986), pp. 413-494.

[2] Ibid

[3] Lee, Rensselaer W.III, *The White Labyrinth: Cocaine trafficking and political power in the Andea Countries.*, A Foreign Policy Research Institute book, 1989, preface.

[4] McCoy, Alfred W., *The Politics of Heroin*, 1991, p. 486.

[5] Lee, 1989, preface

[6] A Cali cocaine cartel leader surrenders after negotiations, *The Miami Herald*, March 13, 1994, p. 21A.

[7] U.S. suspends sharing of anti-drug evidence, *The Miami Herald*, March 20, 1994, p. 27A.

[8] In Colombia, a hero of the drug war loses some of his luster, *The Miami Herald*, April 4, 1994, p. 1A.

[9] Mestre, Ramon., Decriminalize drugs?, *The Miami Herald*, Viewpoints, March 3, 1995, p. 19.

[10] McCoy, p.20.

[11] Latin America Roundup, *The Miami Herald*, Aug. 7, 1991, p. 14A.

NOTES

[12] Drugs Encroach on a Last Line of Defense for the U.S., by Douglas Farah, *The Washington Post National Weekly Edition*, April 10-16, 1995, p. 17.

[13] McCoy, pp. 456-457.

[14] Marquis, Christopher, *The Miami Herald*, Mar. 13, 1991, p. 7A.

[15] Marquis,Christopher and Sheridan, Mary Beth, Stung by drug criticism, Colombia says it may spurn aid, *The Miami Herald*, March 2, 1995, p.11A.

[16] Lippman, Thomas W., Vietnam War was wrong, ex-defense chief writes, *Washington Post Service, reprinted in The Miami Herald*, April 9, 1995, p. 14A.

[17] Nadelmann, Ethan A., Should We Legalize Drugs? History Answers Yes., *American Heritage*, February/March 1993, p. 48.

[18] Friedman, Prof. Milton, The Drug War as a Socialist Enterprise, keynote address presented at the Fifth International Conference on Drug Policy Reform in Washington, D.C., on Nov. 16, 1991. Reprinted in, Friedman & Szasz, *On Liberty and Drugs*, edited and with a Preface by Arnold S. Trebach and Kevin B. Zeese, 1992, pp. 49-55.

[19] *The Defense Monitor*, Center for Defense Information., Vol. XXI. Number 1, p.1

[20] Losing the war on drugs, *The Miami Herald*, May 14, I995, p. 2A.

Chapter 5

[1] Fifth Column, *American Peoples Encyclopedia*, 1953., p. 8-524.

[2] Long, Robert Emmet, editor, *Drugs in America*, The Reference Shelf, Volume 65, Number 4, 1993, p.131.

[3] China, *The Miami Herald*, June 27, 1992, p-7A.

[4] Long, pp. 136-37.

[5] Ibid, p. 212.

[6] Ibid, p. 37.

[7] Undercover drug sting rattles mall shoppers, *The Miami Herald*, July 7, 1992, p. 2B.

[8] Friedman, Milton and Szasz, Thomas S., *On Liberty and Drugs*, p. 79.

[9] Court upholds limits on seizure of drug property, *The Miami Herald*, June 1, 1995, p. 4A.

[10] Bennett, William J., *Mopping Up After the Legalizers*, Speech before the Harvard University Kennedy School of Government, Dec. 11, 1989, reprinted in, *The Crisis in Drug Prohibition*, David Boaz, editor, 1990.

[11] Long, p.165.

179

NOTES

[12] Take charge of your pain, by Mary Batten, *Modern Maturity*, January-February 1995, p. 35 (5 pages.)

[13] Use of pot in AIDS study stonewalled, by Sally Lehrman, *San Francisco Examiner*, reprinted in *The Albuquerque Tribune*, February 24, 1995, p. B6.

[14] Friedman and Szasz, pp. 39-40.

[15] *Possibilities, The Magazine of Hope*, Crystal Cathedral Ministries, March/April 1991, pp. 8-12.

Chapter 6

[1] Shannon, Elaine, *Desperados: Latin Drug Lords, U.S. Lawmakers and the War America Can't Win*, 1988, p. IX.

[2] The Cocaine Habit, *Scientific American*, May 4, 1895, p. 283.

[3] Allen, Frederick Lewis, *Only Yesterday*, 1931, Chapter. 5.

[4] Tom Brokaw on *NBC Nightly News*, September 23, 1994.

[5] Roberts, Sam, *Who We Are: A Portrait of America Based on the Latest U.S. Census*, 1993, p. 190.

[6] Ibid., p. 209.

[7] Covey, Stephen R., *The Seven Habits of Highly Effective People*, 1989, p. 18.

[8] Doyle, Charlotte L., *Explorations in Psychology*, 1987, p. 399.

[9] Roberts, pp. 49-50.

[10] Lebergott, Stanley, *The Americans: An Economic Record*, 1984, p. 368.

[11] Health agency: Time to get tough on cigarette sales to kids and teens, *The Miami Herald*, July 10, 1992, p. 17A.

[12] Officials: Americans are healthier, *The Albuquerque Tribune*, April 12, 1995, p. A9.

[13] Binge drinking the rage at 'party' colleges, *The Miami Herald*, April 6, 1995, p. 11A.

[14] *Final Report of the National Commission on Drug Free Schools*, Bennett, William J. & Cavazos, Lauro F., Co-chairmen, September 1990.

[15] Ibid., p. 73.

[16] Shannon, p. X.

[17] Falco, Mathea, *The Making of a Drug Free America--Programs That Work*, pp. 36-38. Life Skills Training (LST), was designed in the late 1970s by Dr. Gilbert J. Botvin at Cornell University Medical College in New York City. Students Taught Awareness and Resistance (STAR), was developed in the early 1980s at the University of Southern California's Institute for Health Promotion and Disease Prevention Research.

NOTES

18 Reaves, John and Austin, James B., *How to find Help for a Troubled Kid*, 1991, p. 175.

19 Doyle, p. 389.

20 Ibid., pp. 388-89.

21 Random Thoughts, *The Miami Herald*, Sunday July 25, 1993, p. 1C.

22 Covey, p.32.

23 Friedman, Milton & Szasz, Thomas S., *On Liberty and Drugs*, 1992, p. 52.

24 Ibid, p. 54.

25 Williams, Terry, *The Cocaine Kids, The Inside Story of a Teenage Drug Ring*, 1989, pp. 132-33.

Chapter 7

1 Allen, Frederick Lewis, *Only Yesterday*, 1931, p. 245.

2 How America Lost Its First Drug War, by Daniel Kagan, *Insight*, November 20, 1989, p.74.

3 Ibid., p. 68.

4 Gold, Mark S., *The Good News About Drugs and Alcohol: Curing, Treating, and Preventing Substance Abuse in the New Age of Biopsychiatry*, 1991, & Falco, Mathea, *The Making of a Drug Free America--Programs That Work*, 1992.

5 Musto, David F., *The American Disease*, pp.65, 303, n. 36, 304, n. 37.

6 Falco, p.187.

7 Recovery High keeps a door open in Althea's life, by Harrison Fletcher, *The Albuquerque Tribune*, May 24, 1995, p. A2.

8 UNM drug center to lose 31 workers, by Doug Brown, *The Albuquerque Tribune*, May 24, 1995, p. A12.

9 Spreading The Word That Drugs Don't Work At Work, from *ADVANCES*, the national newsletter of the Robert Wood Johnson Foundation, Winter 1995, p. 12.

10 Falco, p. 191.

11 Ibid., p. 177.

12 Sober Thoughts: Letters to the Editor, *New York Magazine*, May 29, 1995, p. 8.

13 Allen, p. 283.

14 Legalize drugs or get tough on them, Gingrich urges, *The Miami Herald*, July 15, 1995, p. 3A.

NOTES

[15] Brecher, Edward M. & the Editors of Consumer Reports, *Licit and Illicit Drugs*, 1972, pp. 120-128.

[16] How to Hold Your Own in a Drug Legalization Debate, *Handbook of the Drug Enforcement Administration,* August 1994.

[17] *The Miami Herald*, Friday, June 25, 1993, p. 5A.

[18] *Holy Bible*, King James Version, Proverbs, chapter 20, verse 1.

[19] Nahas, Gabriel G., *Cocaine:The Great White Plague.*, pp. 42, 255, n. 13.

[20] Sixty Minutes, *A CBS news magazine feature*, May 1, 1994. A report by Leslie Stahl showed the ridiculous situation of government disability payments to alcoholics and drug addicts on the streets that resulted from the Supreme Court decision declaring addiction a disease.

[21] Football Alcohol Crackdown, *The Miami Herald*, July 13, 1991, p. 3D.

Chapter 8

[1] Musto, David F., *The American Disease*, pp. 2, 16 and 286, n. 39.

[2] Ibid, p. 293, n. 43.

[3] Musto, David F, *The American Disease*, p. 42.--Dr. Hamilton Wright, a Delegate to the Opium Commission that met in Shanghai in 1909, conducted a national survey for the State Department in 1909, of police departments, prisons, boards of health, pharmaceutical distributors and drug manufacturers to determine the prevailing use and control of opiates. He testified on his report before Congress on 31 May 1910.

[4] Ibid, pp. 42, 292, n. 40

[5] How America Lost Its First Drug War, by Daniel Kagan, *Insight*, November 20, 1989, p. 12. David T. Courtwright, professor of history at the University of North Florida, is the author of *Dark Paradise: Opiate Addiction in America Before 1940.*

[6] Falco, Mathea, *The Making of a Drug Free America--Programs that Work*, pp. 11, 223, n. 25.

[7] Hard-core Use of Cocaine and Heroin Seems to Be Softening, by John M. Goshke, *The Washington Post National Weekly Edition*, June 5-11, 1995, p. 37.

[8] Figures courtesy of Diane Martin, Public Information officer, Headquarters, Drug Enforcement Administration, Washington, D.C.

[9] Friedman, Milton and Szasz, Thomas S., *On Liberty and Drugs*, 1992, pp. 56-57.

[10] Musto, David F., *The American Disease,* p.323, n. 62.

[11] Ibid, p. 116.

[12] Ibid, p. 246.

[13] Musto, David F., *The American Disease,* pp., 24-68. These two chapters,--(2) Diplomats and Reformers, and, (3) The Harrison Act-- give you an accurate description of the maneuvering and the politics that went into legislating the prohibition of narcotics and cocaine. Dr. Musto did such thorough research, going to the original source documents, including personal letters between many of the participants, that one gets an excellent feel for the motives and the personalities of many of the principal players. Eighty years after the fact, one has the experience that he is reading the story of an excellent investigative reporter who was on the scene at that moment.

[14] Robbins, Lee N., The Vietnam Drug User Returns (Washington, D.C.: Government Printing Office, 1973), and Falco, p. 182.

[15] Falco, p. 182.

[16] Ibid, pp. 24-26.

[17] Ibid, p. 182.

[18] Ibid, p. 18.

[19] Wilson, James Q., Against the Legalization of Drugs, *Commentary,* Feb. 21-28, 1990. Reprinted in *Drugs in America*, edited by Long, pp. 161-177.

[20] Long, p.185.

[21] Cashing in on a heroin epidemic, *The Miami Herald*, April 5, 1994, p. 4A.

[22] Novello, Antonia C., Surgeon General: Speech to Texas Commission on Alcohol and Drug Abuse, July 13, 1992.

[23] Ads made smokers quit faster, study shows, *The Miami Herald*, Monday, January 18, 1993, p. 4A.

[24] Allen, Frederick Lewis, *Only Yesterday*, 1931, p. 247.

[25] Buying prescription drugs with no Rx, by Derek Reveron, *The Miami Herald*, May 17, 1992, p. 1A.

Chapter 9

[1] Covey, Stephen R., *The Seven Habits of Highly Effective People*, 1989, p. 309.

[2] Musto, David F., *The American Disease,* 1987, p. 59. Also see, Musto, Opium, Cocaine, and Marijuana in American History, *Scientific American*, July 1991, p.45.

[3] Friedman, Milton, *The Drug War as a Socialist Enterprise*, keynote address presented at the Fifth International Conference on Drug Policy Reform in Washington, D.C., on November 16, 1991.

---

[4] Thinking Seriously About Alternatives to Drug Prohibition, by Ethan A. Nadelmann, *Daedalus,* Summer 1992, Volume 121:3, p. 88.

[5] How to Legalize, an interview with Princeton professor, Ethan Nadelmann, by Emily Yoffe, *Mother Jones*, Feb./Mar., 1990, pp. 18,19.

[6] Musto, *The American Disease,* 1987, pp. 103, 104. Also: Musto, Opium, Cocaine and Marijuana in American History, 1991, p. 45; and Benjamin, Daniel K., and Miller, Roger Leroy, *Undoing Drugs--Beyond Legalization*, 1991, pp. 6-7.

[7] Eight drug gang leaders convicted of 10 murders, *The Miami Herald*, May 16, 1995, p. 4A.

[8] 'Drug court' is alternative to jail time, by Gil Griffin, *The Albuquerque Tribune,* May 24, 1995.

[9] The Cronkite Report, "The Drug Dilemma: War or Peace?", *Discovery* television channel, June 20, 1995.

[10] Nahas, Gabriel G., *Cocaine: The Great White Plague,* 1989, p. 239.

[11] Ibid., p. 247.

[12] Musto, *The American Disease,* 1987, p. 252.

[13] Nahas, *Cocaine: The Great White Plague,* 1989, p. 244.

[14] Ibid., p. 247.

[15] Musto, *The American Disease,* 1987 p. 303, n. 36.

[16] Roper, William L., Director, Centers for Disease Control, *Linking Science, Policy and Practice:* Address to the Prevention '92 Conference on March 24, 1992, in Baltimore Maryland.

Chapter 10

[1] Chicago Drug Gang, *ABC Nightly News* with Peter Jennings, September 29, 1994.

Conclusion Notes

[1] Monopolizing Family Values, by E. J. Dionne, Jr., *The Washington Post National Weekly Edition*, June 5-11, 1995, p. 29.

[2] Covey, Stephen R., *Seven Habits of Highly Effective People*, 1989, p. 319.

INDEX

INDEX

INDEX

Opium, 12
    Conference at Hague, 19
    smoking prohibited, 19

P

Parke-Davis Company, 15
patent medicines, 12, 15
Percodan, 137
Peru, 41
pharmaceutical distribution system, 76
pharmacies, 12
Playboy magazine, 25
Pope Leo XIII, 15
prescription dispensing of cocaine &
    heroin, 110
Prohibition, 10, 20, 23
prohibition of narcotics, 20
psychoactive drugs, 12
public health clinics, 16
Pure Food and Drug Act, 18, 35, 118

R

Reagan Administration, 71
Reno, Attorney General Janet, 41, 52
Report on Drug-Free Schools, 90
Reveron, Derek, 137
Roaring 20's, 21
Roosevelt, Franklin D., 23
Roosevelt, Pres. Theodore, 29, 164
Roper, Dr. William L., 154
rum-running, 20

S

Saddam Hussein, 117
Schuller, Dr. Robert H., 79
Schwarzkopf, Gen. Norman, 49
Sears Roebuck, 12
Serturner, Frederick W. A., 14
sexual promiscuity, 25
Shepard, Senator Morris, 57
Smith, Al, 23
Social Security Administration
    SSI disability payments, 114
Soldier's disease, 14

Soviet Union, 38
speakeasies, 20
State Department, 19
Students Taught A & R (STAR), 93
Suarez, Roberto, 51
Sunday, Billy, 78
Supreme Court, 20, 114

T

Taft, William Howard,
    U.S. Governor General of the
    Philippines, 29
Temperance Movement, 17, 30
Terry, Surgeon Gen. Luther, 129
The Commission, 21
The Noble Experiment, 20
Treasury Department, 23

V

Vietnamese gangs, 67
Vin Mariani, 15

W

Washington, Pres. George, 163
Weinberger, Caspar, 61
Wets, 23
Wickersham commission, 10
White Cross, 22
Williams, Terry, 97
Wilson, Pres. Woodrow, 163
Wilson, Professor James Q., 125
World War II, 24
Wright, Dr. Hamilton, 33, 119
    1910 Report to Congress, 119

Y

youth gangs, 40

About the author

Lieutenant Colonel Robert H. Dowd, USAF-Ret. is eminently qualified by background, education, and training to dissect the U.S. government's "War on Drugs." A career Air Force officer for 30 years, Colonel Dowd first learned the capabilities—and limitations—of military force while flying 50 missions in the European Theater of Operations as a B-26 Marauder bomber pilot during World War II. His post-World War II service included the Berlin Airlift, and rescue missions in the Arctic. Colonel Dowd later served in Korea, and was assigned to an Air Commando squadron flying gunships during the Vietnam War.

In addition to his flying skills, Colonel Dowd's analytical abilities gained him a prized research assignment with Air Force Cambridge Research Laboratories in Massachusetts, and later served as project officer for a major research project during the United States' last atmospheric nuclear test in 1962. He was also a key staff member on the Department of Defense joint staff serving in the NASA Mission Control Center in support of the Apollo lunar missions.

A graduate of Florida State University and the prestigious Air War College, Colonel Dowd first became concerned about the government's flawed drug policy during his overseas assignments in the 1960s. Later, when President Nixon declared a War on Drugs in 1972, Colonel Dowd began examining the similarities between the government's drug war strategy and the military tactics that failed in Vietnam.

Colonel Dowd's compassion for the victims of the War on Drugs and his concern for the nation's future prompted him to research the historical roots of the U.S. drug problem and devise a better solution in his book, *The Enemy Is Us.*

Before undertaking the research and writing of this book, Colonel Dowd was an officer in one of Florida's largest banking corporations. He is a native of Miami, Florida, and resides there with his wife, Rosemary.